Praying the PSALMS
Changes Things

Praying the
PSALMS
Changes Things

Lloyd Hildebrand

BRIDGE LOGOS

Alachua, Florida 32615

Bridge-Logos

Alachua, FL 32615 USA

Praying The Psalms Changes Things
by Lloyd Hildebrand

Printed in the United States of America.

Library of Congress Catalog Card Number: 2014935107

International Standard Book Number:
 978-1-61036-126-2

Unless otherwise noted, all Scripture quotations are from the King James Version of the Holy Bible.

VP 08-13-14

DEDICATION

To all who are dedicated to spreading God's Word, including Choice Books, all our distributors, and the staff of Bridge-Logos, Inc. Thank you for your hard work in building God's kingdom on Earth.

Contents

INTRODUCTION

I LOVE the Psalms! The Book of Psalms is the central book of the Bible, and it is the place to go when you are hurting or struggling with any negative situations and feelings, because the Psalms are filled with healing truths. From the Psalms you can glean glistening nuggets from the goldmines of God and find healing for your heart and soul.

The Psalms reveal God's heart to us. Filled with promises from Him, these 150 chapters tell us what He wants for us and how to obtain His blessings in our lives. As you read the Psalms, you will see how much God loves you.

The word "Psalms" literally means "songs," and the 150 lyric songs it contains lift the human heart in worship and adoration of God, our Creator. Through the Psalms God addresses every human emotion and need. They reveal the attributes of God to us, and they show us how He wants us to live.

People read the Psalms more than they read any other book of the Bible. Jesus made use of the Psalms in His teachings and Peter incorporated messages from the Psalms in his first gospel sermon. Many of the early martyrs of the Church went to their deaths quoting the Psalms. John Huss was one of these, and when he was condemned, he quoted these words from Psalm

31: "Bow down thine ear to me; deliver me speedily: be thou my strong rock, for an house of defence to save me. For thou art my rock and my fortress; therefore for thy name's sake lead me, and guide me. Pull me out of the net that they have laid privily for me: for thou art my strength. Into thine hand I commit my spirit: thou hast redeemed me, O Lord God of truth" (Psalm 31:1-5).

Do you long for God's presence? Do you want to draw near to Him? Do you want to hear Him speaking to you? Go to the Psalms, and there you will experience His presence, love, and joy. Are you filled with intense emotions that you do not know how to express? Let the Psalms help you.

In the Psalms you will discover answers to many of life's dilemmas and struggles, and you will see your sins, sorrows, aspirations, dreams, desires, hopes, joys, failures, and victories reflected there. W. E. Gladstone said, "All the wonders of Greek civilization heaped together are less wonderful than is this simple Book of the Psalms."

Praying the Psalms Changes Things is focused on prayers that have been built directly from the Psalms. They are arranged topically so that you can find issues that you are dealing with in your own life. They are personal so that you can express your own feelings as you pray. They are uplifting because, "All scripture is given by inspiration of God, and is profitable for doctrine, for reproof, for correction, for instruction in righteousness, that the man of God may be perfect, thoroughly furnished unto all good works" (2 Timothy 3:16, 17).

How does praying the Psalms change things? It helps you to know the truth about the situations and circumstances of your life. It builds your faith. It gives you a glimpse of God, who is always there for you. It helps you to grow spiritually. As a result of these blessings and many more you will see things changing around you, because your view of those things will change radically as you pray.

The Psalms were written by several men. David wrote seventy-three. Asaph (the music director during the reigns of David and Solomon) wrote twelve. Eleven were written by the sons of Korah (twelve Levites who served in the Temple), two were written by Solomon (a son of David who became his successor as the King of Israel), one was written by Moses (the patriarch who led the Israelites out of Egypt), one was written by Ethan (a companion of Asaph and Heman in temple worship), and one was written by Heman (a contemporary of David and Asaph. He was known as "the singer").The remaining fifty Psalms are anonymous, but many think that David was their author.

In the Psalms we find a description of human responses to God. They also reveal realistic human feelings and the way we respond to life's situations, including its problems and inequities. The Psalmists show us that the most profound prayer of all is simply, "Help!"

Praying the Psalms will change many things, but the most important thing it will change is YOU.

PART I

<hr>

JESUS IN THE PSALMS

Jesus loved the Psalms and frequently quoted from them. He said, "These are the words which I spake unto you, while I was yet with you, that all things must be fulfilled, which were written in the law of Moses, and in the prophets, and in the psalms, concerning me" (Luke 24:44).

In this verse we see Jesus revealing that many of the things that were written in the Psalms and the prophetic books of the Bible pertained to Him. Psalms that refer to Jesus hundreds of years before He was born are known as Messianic Psalms, and these are actually Messianic prophecies that foretell what would happen through the life, death, and resurrection of Jesus.

Some of those Messianic Psalms are discussed in this chapter.

THE KING OF KINGS AND LORD OF LORDS (PSALM 2)

One thousand years before Christ walked on this Earth many of the Psalms talked about Him. These Psalms could not have referred to anyone but Him. In Psalm 2, for example, we read about Jesus as our divine King. His reign is universal. The Psalmist writes, "Yet have I set my king [the Lord Jesus Christ] upon my holy hill of Zion. I will declare the decree; the Lord hath said unto me, Thou art my Son; this day have I begotten thee. Ask of me, and I shall give thee the heathen for thine inheritance, and the uttermost parts of the earth for thy possession."

The Kingdom of God is to be founded and maintained by the Son of God, His anointed King, the King of kings and the Lord of lords, and He will receive the heathen and the entire Earth as His possession.

Do you see how the reign of Christ is universal and all-powerful? Psalm 2 goes on: "Thou shalt break them with a rod of iron; thou shalt dash them in pieces like a potter's vessel." The power of the Lord Jesus is unlimited.

To "kiss the Son" is to give Him homage and to worship Him. As we learn to put our trust in Him, we will experience temporal and eternal happiness. We will be truly blessed. Let us worship Him in the beauty of holiness. Let us truly "kiss the Son."

John wrote, "And he hath on his vesture and on his

thigh a name written, King of kings and Lord of lords" (Revelation 19:16). Is He the Lord of your life?

THE MAJESTY OF GOD (PSALM 8)

This glorious Psalm was written by David, and it magnifies the name of the Lord and the marvels of His creation. It also reveals the insignificance of human beings. In spite of this insignificance, though, the Psalm assures us that through the Lord Jesus Christ we shall have dominion over God's creation.

David prays, "O Lord our Lord, how excellent is thy name in all the earth!" (Psalm 8:9).

In this Psalm we also see that through Jesus we shall be able to ". . . still the enemy and the avenger" (Psalm 8:2).

It is the blessed name of Jesus that enables us to still the avenger. In James we read, "Submit yourselves therefore to God. Resist the devil, and he will flee from you" (James 4:7).

The name of Jesus gives us great power. He said, "And whatsoever ye shall ask in my name, that will I do, that the Father may be glorified in the Son" (John 14:13). What a wonderful prayer promise this is.

THE GOLDEN PSALM (PSALM 16)

This Psalm is a *Michtam* of David. This Hebrew word is often translated as "the Golden Psalm of David," an appropriate appellation in that this Psalm refers to the Resurrection of Jesus Christ. This Psalm is also known as "the Psalm of the Precious Secret," because in this Psalm we find David writing about the coming Savior.

David writes, "The secret of the Lord is with them that fear him; and he will shew them his covenant" (Psalm 25:14). Our Lord reveals spiritual secrets to His children when we study His Word and listen for His voice.

Jerome wrote (about Psalm 16), "The Psalm pertains to Christ, who speaks in it. . . .It is the voice of our King, which he utters in the human nature that he had assumed, but without detracting from his divine nature. . . .The Psalm pertains to His passion."

In Acts 2 we read these words of commentary on Psalm 16 from the Apostle Peter: "For David speaketh concerning him, I foresaw the Lord always before my face, for he is on my right hand, that I should not be moved. . . .He seeing this before spake of the resurrection of Christ, that his soul was not left in hell, neither his flesh did see corruption. This Jesus hath God raised up, whereof we are all witnesses" (Acts 2:25-32).

It's amazing, but David was writing about the Resurrection of Jesus Christ hundreds of years before He died. The power of Christ's resurrection remains with us today. Paul writes, "That I may know him, and the power of his resurrection, and the fellowship of his sufferings, being made conformable unto his death" (Philippians 3:10).

Do you know Him and the power of His resurrection?

THE PASSION OF CHRIST (PSALM 22)

In this Psalm of David we see a foreshadowing of the Crucifixion of Jesus, and Jesus quoted from this Psalm when He was hanging on the cross: "My God, my God, why hast thou forsaken me?" (Psalm 22:1). It is almost as if David was present at the Crucifixion of Jesus when he wrote this vivid description of this vitally important future event: "All they that see me laugh me to scorn: they shoot out the lip, they shake the head, saying, 'He trusted on the Lord that he would deliver him: let him deliver him, seeing he delighted in him" (Psalm 22:7–8).

Jesus was sneered at, and His hands and feet were pierced, as David described in verse 16. As the Psalm goes on, we hear the voice of Jesus speaking: "They cast my garments among them, and cast lots upon my vesture" (Psalm 22:18).

Other verses in this chapter apply directly to the Crucifixion of Jesus as well. Jesus quoted from this Psalm as He was dying on the cross. (See Matthew 27:46 and Mark 15:34.)

The Prophet Isaiah gave us a Messianic prophecy about the Crucifixion as well: "He is despised and rejected of men; a man of sorrows, and acquainted with grief: and we hid as it were our faces from him; he was despised, and we esteemed him not. Surely he hath borne our griefs, and carried our sorrows: yet we did esteem him stricken, smitten of God, and afflicted. But he was wounded for our transgressions, he was bruised for our iniquities: the chastisement of our peace was upon him; and with his stripes we are healed. All we like sheep have gone astray; we have turned every one to his own way; and the Lord hath laid on him the iniquity of us all. He was oppressed, and he was afflicted, yet he opened not his mouth: he is brought as a lamb to the slaughter, and as a sheep before her shearers is dumb, so he openeth not his mouth" (Isaiah 53:3-7).

Jesus died for you so that you would not perish but have everlasting life, as we read in John 3:16: "For God so loved the world, that he gave his only begotten Son, that whosoever believeth in him should not perish, but have everlasting life."

This truth must not be overlooked, for it will set you free.

THE BRIDEGROOM AND THE BRIDE (PSALM 45)

This Psalm is the royal marriage song of Jesus (the Bridegroom) and the Church (His bride). In this chapter we see the Messiah anticipating the Marriage of the Lamb that was written about by the Apostle John: "Let us be glad and rejoice, and give honour to him; for the marriage of the Lamb is come, and his wife hath made herself ready" (Revelation 19:7).

The Psalmist begins by describing the King (Jesus): "Thou art fairer than the children of men: grace is poured into thy lips: therefore God hath blessed thee forever. Gird thy sword upon thy thigh, O most mighty, with thy glory and thy majesty" (Psalm 45:2-3).

Later in the same chapter he writes about the Bride of Christ (the Church) as follows: "So shall the king greatly desire thy beauty: for he is thy Lord; and worship thou him" (Psalm 45:11).

The marriage is described most beautifully by the Psalmist. He writes: "The king's daughter is all glorious within: her clothing is of wrought gold. She shall be brought unto the king in raiment of needlework: the virgins her companions that follow her shall be brought unto thee. With gladness and rejoicing shall they be brought: they shall enter into the king's palace."

What a beautiful scene, and, as the Body of Christ, we will be there! Paul writes, ". . .Christ also loved the church, and gave himself for it; that he might sanctify and cleanse it with the washing of water by the word, that he might present it to himself a glorious church, not having spot, or wrinkle, or any such thing; but that it should be holy and without blemish" (Ephesians 5:25-27).

What a time of rejoicing that will be!

THE MESSIAH'S REIGN (PSALM 72)

This Psalm was written by Solomon, but it describes the reign of One who is greater than Solomon. It tells us that Jesus will judge His people with righteousness, save the children of the needy, break the oppressor in pieces, etc.

The Lord Jesus Christ's reign will be characterized by deliverance, protection, redemption, and dominion. "His name shall endure for ever: his name shall be continued as long as the sun: and men shall be blessed in him: all nations shall call him blessed" (Psalm 72:17).

Jesus, as Paul points out, has been raised from the dead and is now seated in the heavenly places. (See Ephesians 1:21.) The Great Apostle writes, "Wherefore God also hath highly exalted him, and given him a name which is above every name: that at the name of Jesus every knee should bow, of things in heaven, and things in earth, and things under the earth; and that every tongue should confess that Jesus Christ is Lord, to the glory of God the Father" (Philippians 2:9-11).

Blessed be His holy name!

AN ENDLESS REIGN (PSALM 89)

In this Psalm God gives an oath to David: "I have made a covenant with my chosen, I have sworn unto David my servant. Thy seed will I establish forever, and build up thy throne to all generations. Selah. And the heavens shall praise thy wonders, O Lord: thy faithfulness also in the congregation of the saints" (Psalm 89:3-5).

Jesus descended through the seed of David who was promised an enduring kingdom. "Thy seed will I establish forever, and build up thy throne to all generations" (Psalm 89:4).

The seed of David (Jesus) will reign forever and

ever. Hallelujah! His throne will endure through all generations. From His throne on High, He ever lives to make intercession for us. (See Hebrews 7:25.)

He is praying for you even now. Robert Murray M'Cheyne writes, "If I could hear Christ praying for me in the next room, I would not fear a million enemies. Yet distance makes no difference. He is praying for me."

THE COMING KING AND OUR HIGH PRIEST (PSALM 110)

Jesus is coming again, and this Psalm of David tells us a lot about it. God will cause the enemies of Jesus to become His footstool. Jesus will rule over those enemies. He is a high priest forever. David writes, "The Lord hath sworn, and will not repent, Thou art a priest for ever after the order of Melchizedek" (Psalm 110: 4).

The Psalmist shows that Jesus will be a priest like Melchizedek. (See Hebrews 5:6.) He is our Advocate, our Intercessor, and our Mediator. As our High Priest, He represents us to God the Father.

Our Savior, Lord, High Priest, and King will return! Anticipation is building around the world for His coming. Praise God for this blessed hope we have in Him.

JESUS' HYMN OF PRAISE (PSALM 118)

So many verses within this Messianic Psalm are very familiar and quite quotable:

Verse 1: *"O give thanks unto the Lord; for he is good: because his mercy endureth forever."*

Verse 5: *"I called upon the Lord in distress: the Lord answered me, and set me in a large place."*

Verse 6: *"The Lord is on my side; I will not fear: what can man do unto me?"*

Verse 9: *"It is better to trust in the Lord than to put confidence in man."*

Verse 14: *"The Lord is my strength and song, and is become my salvation."*

Verse 17: *"I shall not die, but live, and declare the works of the Lord."*

Verse 23: *"This is the Lord's doing; it is marvelous in our eyes."*

Verse 24: *"This is the day which the Lord hath made; we will rejoice and be glad in it."*

Praise God for this Messianic Psalm, which shows the gratitude of the Lord Jesus to His Father, and gives us so many blessings for us to reflect upon.

His mercy endures forever, and He hears and answers our prayers. He is always on our side—the Lord who is always there for us. Because He is with us, there is no reason to fear. As we learn to trust Him, we will discover that He is our strength and our song. He has become our salvation.

As we live, let us declare His works to others, for

His works are His doing, and they are marvelous in our eyes.

Remember, this is the day that the Lord has made. Let us rejoice and be glad in it.

GOD'S UNBREAKABLE PROMISE
(PSALM 132)

God gave a promise to David that there would be an inheritor of his throne who would reign forever. That inheritor is Jesus, and this Psalm reiterates this wonderful promise.

It also outlines many of the wonderful things that the King of kings will do. He will abundantly bless us and satisfy us. We will shout aloud for joy.

It is fitting to close out this chapter with a personalized prayer from Psalm 132: "Lord, thank you for remembering David in all his afflictions. Thank you that he was devoted to finding a habitation for you [the Temple which his son Solomon built]. As David did, I will go into your tabernacle and I will worship at your footstool. Arise, O Lord, into your rest. Let me be clothed with your righteousness. I will shout for joy because of who you are and all you've done. It is my heart's desire to keep your testimonies and your covenant and to teach your truths to others. Thank you for choosing me to be your dwelling place. Thank you for abundantly blessing me and mine. In Jesus' name I pray, Amen."

PART II

DAVID—A MAN AFTER GOD'S OWN HEART

[God] said, I have found David the son of Jesse,
A man after mine own heart,
which shall fulfill all my will.
(Acts 13:22)

David was a shepherd boy, a valiant warrior, an astute leader, a poet, a singer, a husband, a father, and a king. He was a very complex man who possessed many strengths and weaknesses. He loved God, the world, beauty, poetry, and music. He loved to worship God and felt very close to Him, and this is reflected poignantly in many of the Psalms. Undoubtedly, David was a great man, and his failings and sins help us to understand him more clearly. He was fully human, but he possessed great courage, faith, and resiliency.

His story is told in 1 Samuel 16–31, 2 Samuel, and 1 Kings 1 and 2, and what a story it is. David was the son of Jesse, a prosperous and greatly respected sheep farmer in the area around Bethlehem. When he was a boy, David was anointed by Samuel and the Spirit of God came upon him in a mighty way. Samuel chose David to be the successor to King Saul.

King Saul suffered from depression. Members of his court felt that music might help to soothe his nerves, so young David was brought in to his chambers to sing and play the harp. The lad's music calmed the king, and the evil spirits that were plaguing his mind left him. During this period David tended his father's sheep in the hills around Bethlehem, and he composed songs and poetry while doing so.

As a youth, David killed a lion and a bear. His next victim would be the giant Goliath of the Philistines. David hurled a stone from his sling that struck the giant in the forehead, stunned him, and knocked him to the ground. David rushed forward and decapitated Goliath. These acts certainly impressed Saul and his son, Jonathan, and David and Jonathan became the best of friends from that point on.

David became a highly respected military leader. Eventually, King Saul grew very envious of David, because the young man was receiving so much more adulation than he was. This angered the king very deeply and he tried to kill David on two different occasions. He failed in both of these attempts; he then began to send David on dangerous missions. He sent men to kill him, and soon David was on the run—a fugitive who was being pursued by agents of the king.

Though David had several opportunities to kill Saul, he always chose not to do so and to keep on honoring the king. When the king was eventually killed by a young Amalekite, David ordered the assassin to be killed, and he fell into deep grief over King Saul's death. He felt grief for his good friend Jonathan, the son of the king. David wrote, "I am distressed for you, my brother Jonathan; very pleasant have you been to me; your love to me was wonderful, passing the love of women" (2 Samuel 1:26).

After the death of Saul, David became the King of Judah, the largest and most powerful of all the tribes of Israel. The northern and southern parts of Israel needed to be reunited, and this was David's next challenge. David was thirty years old when the reunification took place, and he ruled over the reunified Israel for forty years.

King David made Jerusalem the capital city of Israel. He also turned the city into the religious center of Israel. The king began to expand the nation by conquering other tribes. During this period David saw Bathsheba when she was bathing and he was greatly attracted to her. He made love to her, and she became pregnant. Her husband, Uriah, was killed in conflict after David had him sent to the front lines.

David took Bathsheba to be his wife. She bore him a son who died not long afterward. The couple had a second son, and his name was Solomon. Absalom was David's third son who eventually turned against his father.

The expanded kingdom was very prosperous and became the leading country in the Middle East. However, as a result of Absalom's rebellion against his father, David became a fugitive once more. Absalom and his forces attacked Jerusalem, and the king fled. In the ensuing warfare, Absalom was killed.

After much warfare, the rule of King David was reestablished. As he grew old, he spent much time in prayer, eventually withdrew from fighting altogether, and abdicated the throne in favor of Solomon. After a reign of forty years, David ". . . slept with his fathers, and was buried in the city of David" (1 Kings 2:10).

"The sweet Psalmist of Israel" (2 Samuel 23:1) went to be with the Lord, but he has been remembered by people ever since as one of the greatest men who ever lived. In many ways his life was enigmatic, and his biographers were careful to show him as a fully human man with many contradictions. Under his leadership the Hebrew nation reached the peak of its military and political strength.

David's Psalms are some of the most memorable poems ever written. The anthology of Hebrew poems and hymns (known as the Psalms) presents many themes:

- Praise and worship
- Trusting God
- Faithfulness
- Joy
- Sorrow
- Grief and mourning
- History
- Bible meditation
- Many others

The Psalms have had a profound influence upon western thought and literature through the ages. They show the importance of close communion with God.

David's Strengths

- He was a courageous and brave warrior
- He always trusted God
- He was a great leader and a military genius
- He was loyal, even to King Saul
- He loved God
- He was a brilliant statesman
- He was a great poet and musician
- He was a faithful friend
- He was handsome
- He was full of faith. (See Hebrews 11:32.)

David's Weaknesses

- He committed adultery with Bathsheba
- He had Uriah the Hittite (Bathsheba's husband) killed
- He violated God's commandment to not take a census of the people
- He was sometimes a lax father who failed to discipline his children when they needed it
- He had a problem with lust
- He was sometimes merciless

David's Accomplishments

- He killed the giant Goliath
- He was victorious over many of Israel's enemies
- He developed a close friendship with Saul's son, Jonathan, that serves as a good model for friendships even today
- He was successful in so many of his endeavors
- He wrote many of the Psalms

King David, though a man of many contrasts, deeply loved God and he was committed to Him. These truths are revealed in many of the Psalms he wrote.

PART III

THE SHEPHERD'S PRAYER
(BASED ON THE SHEPHERD'S PSALM)

Psalm 23 is perhaps the best-known chapter in the Bible. David may have composed this Psalm when he was a shepherd boy. It is filled with images and figures of speech that come from a pastoral setting. Here we have personalized the Psalm and turned it into a personal prayer that can be prayed at any time. This is the type of prayer that you will find in later sections of this book.

Prayer: Lord, I thank you for being my Shepherd, the One who takes care of me and supplies all my needs. Because this is true, I know I shall never want. Thank you for the peace you give to me. You make me lie down in green pastures and you lead me beside the still waters. I love you, Lord.

Thank you for restoring my soul every day and leading me in the paths of righteousness for your name's sake. Even when I walk through the valley of the shadow of death, I will fear no evil, for I know you are with me. Seeing your rod and staff in front of me gives me great comfort.

Thank you for preparing a table before me in the presence of my enemies and for anointing my head with oil. My cup truly overflows.

Surely your goodness and mercy will follow me all the days of my life, and I will dwell in your house forever. Hallelujah!

PART IV

⎯⎯⎯∞⎯⎯⎯

YOU ARE BLESSED!
(PERSONAL BLESSINGS IN THE PSALMS)

Blessed is the man that walks not in the counsel of the ungodly. (Psalm 1:1)

Blessed are all they that put their trust in Him. (Psalm 2:12)

Blessed is he whose transgression is forgiven, whose sin is covered. (Psalm 32:1)

Blessed is the nation whose God is the Lord. (Psalm 33:12)

Blessed is the man that trusts in God. (Psalm 34:8)

Blessed is the person that considers the poor. (Psalm 41:1)

Blessed are they that dwell in God's house. (Psalm 84:4)

Blessed is the man whose strength is in God. (Psalm 84:5)

Blessed is the man whom the Lord chastens and teaches. (Psalm 94:12)

Blessed are they that keep the Lord's testimonies and that seek God with their whole heart. (Psalm 119:2)

PART V

———⚬⚬⚬———

PRAYER NUGGETS FROM THE PSALMIST DAVID

These little prayers from David will strengthen your faith as you pray them from your heart, as he did. Memorize them so that you can pray them from your heart at any time.

Psalm 3:3: You, O Lord, are a shield for me; my glory, and the lifter of my head.

Psalm 4:8: I will lie down in peace and sleep, for you, Lord, make me dwell in safety.

Psalm 5:2-3: Hearken unto the voice of my cry, my King, and my God, for unto you I will pray. You will hear my voice in the morning, O Lord; in the morning I will direct my prayer unto you and will look up.

Psalm 7:1: O Lord my God, in you do I place my trust. Deliver me from all who persecute me.

Psalm 8:9: O Lord, our Lord, how excellent is your name in all the earth!

Psalm 9:1: I will praise you, O Lord, with my whole heart. I will show forth all your marvelous works.

Psalm 13:5-6: I have trusted in your mercy; my heart will rejoice in your salvation.

Psalm 16:11: You will show me the path of life. In your presence there is fullness of joy. At your right hand there are pleasures forevermore.

Psalm 17:8: Keep me as the apple of your eye; hide me under the shadow of your wings.

Psalm 18:1-2: I will love you, O Lord, my strength. You are my rock, my fortress, and my deliverer. You are my God and my strength, and I trust in you. You are my buckler, the horn of my salvation, and my high tower.

Psalm 18:28-30: You will light my candle, and you will enlighten my darkness, for by you I have run through a troop, and by you I have leaped over a wall. Your way is perfect, and your Word is tried.

Psalm 19:14: Let the words of my mouth and the meditation of my heart be acceptable in your sight, O Lord, my strength and my Redeemer.

Psalm 21:13: Be exalted, O Lord, in your own strength. So will I sing and praise your power.

Psalm 25:1-2: *Unto thee, O Lord, do I lift up my soul. O my God, I trust in you. Do not let me be ashamed. Do not let my enemies triumph over me.*

Psalm 25:4-5: *Show me your ways, O Lord; teach me your paths. Lead me in your truth and teach me, for you are the God of my salvation, and on you I wait all day long.*

Psalm 25:21: *Let integrity and uprightness preserve me, for I wait on you.*

Psalm 27:11: *Teach me your way, O Lord, and lead me in a plain path because of my enemies.*

Psalm 30:1-3: *I will extol you, O Lord, for you have lifted me up and have not allowed my enemies to rejoice over me. O Lord my God, I cried unto you and you healed me. O Lord, you have brought up my soul from the grave. You have kept me alive, that I should not go down to the pit.*

Psalm 36:5: *Your mercy, O Lord, is in the heavens and your faithfulness reaches unto the clouds.*

Psalm 36:7-9: *How excellent is your loving-kindness, O God. . . . for the fountain of life is with you. In your light I see light.*

Psalm 38:15: *For in you, O Lord, do I hope. You will hear, O Lord my God.*

Psalm 40:5-8: *Many, O Lord my God, are your wonderful works which you have done. . . . I delight to do your will, O my God. Yes, your law is within my heart.*

Psalm 41:11: *By this I know that you favor me, because my enemy does not triumph over me. And, as for me, you uphold me in my integrity, and set your face before me forever.*

Psalm 51:1-2: *Have mercy upon me, O God, according to your loving-kindness. According to the multitude of your tender mercies, blot out my transgressions. Wash me thoroughly from my iniquity, and cleanse me from my sin.*

Psalm 51:10: *Create in me a clean heart, O God, and renew a right spirit within me.*

Psalm 51:12: *Restore unto me the joy of your salvation, and uphold me with your free spirit.*

Psalm 51:15: *O Lord, open my lips and my mouth shall show forth your praise.*

Psalm 63:1: *O God, you are my God. Early will I seek you. My soul thirsts for you. My flesh longs for you in a dry and thirsty land where no water is.*

Psalm 63:3-4: *Because your loving-kindness is better than life, my lips will praise you. Thus I will bless you for as long as I live. I will lift up my hands in your name.*

Psalm 65:1: *Praise waits for you, O God, in Zion. Unto you shall the vow be performed.*

Psalm 86:10-12: *You are great and you do wondrous things. You are God alone. Teach me your way, O Lord. I will walk in your truth. Unite my heart to fear your name. I will praise you, O Lord my God, with all* *my heart, and I will glorify your name forever.*

Psalm 103:1-3: *Bless the Lord, O my soul, and all that is within me, bless His holy name. Bless the Lord, O my soul, and forget not all His benefits.*

Psalm 108:1-4: *O God, my heart is fixed. I will sing and give praise even with my glory. . . . For your mercy is great above the heavens, and your truth reaches to the clouds.*

Psalm 139:1-4: *O Lord, you have searched me and known me. You know my sitting down and my rising up. You understand my thoughts from afar. You compass my path and my lying down, and you are acquainted with all my ways. There is not a word on my tongue, but you know it altogether.*

Psalm 139:14: *I will praise you, for I am fearfully and wonderfully made. Marvelous are your works. My soul knows this very well.*

Psalm 139:17: *How precious are your thoughts to me, O God! How great is the sum of them.*

Psalm 139:23-24: *Search me, O God, and know my heart: try me, and know my thoughts. See if there is any wicked way in me, and lead me in the everlasting way.*

Psalm 141:2-3: *Let my prayer be set forth before you as incense, and the lifting up of my hands as the evening sacrifice. Set a watch, O Lord, before my mouth. Keep the door of my lips.*

Psalm 143:8: Cause me to hear your loving-kindness in the morning, for in you do I trust. Cause me to know the way in which I should walk, for I lift up my soul to you.

Psalm 143:10-11: Teach me to do your will, for you are my God. Your Spirit is good. Lead me into the land of uprightness. Quicken me, O Lord.

Psalm 145:3: Great is the Lord, and greatly to be praised. Your greatness is unsearchable.

PART VI

———— ∞∞∞ ————

PERSONALIZING THE PSALMS THROUGH PRAYER

Many of the Psalms are personal prayers of adoration, confession, thanksgiving, and supplication. You may pray these as if they are your own personal prayers, and it is very exciting and enlightening to do so.

Other Psalms can be personalized by putting them into the first person singular as if they are coming from your own heart. As you do so, you will want to meditate upon the Psalms and the multitude of truths they contain—truths that you can apply to your own heart.

As you personalize the Psalms in this way, begin by asking yourself these questions:

- Are there any promises for me to claim?
- Are there any truths for me to apply to my own life?
- Are there any errors that I should avoid?
- What does this passage teach me about the Lord Jesus Christ?
- Are there any commandments for me to obey?
- Are there good examples for me to follow or bad examples for me to avoid?

You will soon discover that the Psalms adapt themselves to your personal prayer life in fascinating ways. In your daily quiet time with God start personalizing the Psalms and praying them from your heart. You will be amazed to see how they will change your attitude, your outlook, and your life.

Have you ever found it difficult to pray about your fears, your struggles, your worries, your sins, your sorrows, or your regrets? Let the Psalms help you. As you pray the Psalms, you will hear the voice of the One who created you and inspired the words of the Psalms. He is your faithful, loving Father who always wants the very best for you.

Nearly every passage in the Psalms can be personalized and turned into a prayer. I encourage you to do so now. Apply the truths of each prayer to your heart and life. As you do so, things will change because your attitude toward them will change.

Better yet, you will change in wonderful ways, and, as you continue to pray the Psalms throughout your life, you will be able to stand upon God's promises securely and confidently.

PART VII

PRAYING THE PSALMS

The topical prayers found within this chapter are built directly from the Psalms. They deal with some of the main themes of the Psalms and the needs of the human heart.

1
ABIDING IN THE LORD—
YOUR PLACE OF REFUGE

*He that dwelleth in the secret place of the most
High shall abide under the shadow of the Almighty.*
(Psalm 91:1)

Central Truth: God is your safe place.

Central Focus: The Lord wants you to abide in Him.
To abide means to stay put, to dwell, and to live in
a particular place. Pray that God will always be your
dwelling place, your abode, because abiding in Him
brings rest and joy like nothing else can.

Prayer: O Most High God, help me ever to remember
to dwell in your secret place and to abide under your
shadow. You are my Almighty God, and you are my
refuge and my fortress. In you I will always trust.

Thank you for your many promises of deliverance,
which I claim right now. Thank you for covering me with
your feathers, and allowing me to trust you as I abide
under your wings. Your truth, dear Father, is my shield
and my buckler.

Because of these truths, I will not be afraid of anything,
including the arrow that flies by day or the terror that
comes at night. I will not fear the pestilence that walks
in darkness nor the destruction that wastes at noonday.
There is no reason for me to fear anyone or anything.

Thank you, Father.

Though a thousand may fall at my side and ten thousand at my right hand, I claim your promise that I will be safe. Father, I want to continue to make you my habitation, knowing that as I do so, no evil will befall me and no plague will come near my dwelling. Hallelujah!

Thank you for giving your angels charge over me, to keep me in all my ways. I know they will bear me up in their hands, lest I dash my foot against a stone. Your power enables me to tread upon the lion and adder.

Through your power I will trample all enemies under my feet.

I have set my love upon you, O Lord. Thank you for your promise to deliver me and set me on high because I know your name. When I call upon you, you will answer me. You will be with me in trouble, and you will deliver me and honor me.

Thank you, Abba-Father. It is wonderful to know that you will satisfy me with long life and show me your salvation.

Hear my prayer, O God. Attend unto my prayer. Lead me to the rock that is higher than me. You are a shelter for me and a strong tower from the enemy. Praise your mighty name! I will abide in your tabernacle forever. I will trust in the covering of your wings.

Thank you for allowing me to abide before you forever.

Your mercy and grace preserve me. I will ever sing praise to you. I love you, Lord, and I choose to abide in you forever.

In Jesus' name I pray, Amen.

Scriptures: Psalm 91; Psalm 61.

Personal Affirmation: Abiding in the Lord brings great peace and joy to me. It is my heart's desire to dwell in the secret place of the Most High forever and to abide under the shadow of the Almighty.

New Testament Scripture: "Abide in me, and I in you. As the branch cannot bear fruit of itself, except it abide in the vine; nor more can ye, except ye abide in me" (John 15:5).

Reflection: *"We should be astonished at the goodness of God, stunned that He should bother to call us by name, our mouths wide open at His love, bewildered that at this very moment we are standing on holy ground"* (Brennan Manning).

2
AFFLICTIONS—LEARNING IN TIMES OF DIFFICULTY

Turn thee unto me, and have mercy upon me;
for I am desolate and afflicted.
(Psalm 25:16)

Central Truth: God is with you in all your afflictions.

Central Focus: God is bigger and greater than any affliction I am going through or could ever go through. He will see me through every affliction through His mercy and grace. He will always be with me.

Prayer: Abba-Father, unto you I lift up my soul. I trust in you to see me through this time of affliction. Show me your ways, O Lord, and teach me your paths. Lead me in your truth and teach me, for you are the God of my salvation, and I wait on you throughout this day.

Thank you for your tender mercies and your loving-kindnesses. They have always been with me. My eyes are ever turned toward you, Lord God. Turn unto me and have mercy upon me, for I am desolate and afflicted. The troubles of my heart are enlarged. Please bring me out of the current distress I am going through.

Look upon my affliction and my pain. Forgive all my sins. O keep my soul and deliver me. Let me not be ashamed, for I place my trust in you.

Thank you, Father, for regarding my affliction and caring about me. Blessed be your name from everlasting to everlasting. Thank you for your Word, which gives me great comfort in this time of affliction. Consider my affliction, Father, and deliver me, for I do not forget your law.

Plead my cause, and deliver me. Quicken me according to your Word. Great are your tender mercies, O Lord. Quicken me according to your judgments. Your Word is true from the beginning, and every one of your righteous judgments endure forever. I rejoice at your Word, as one who finds great spoil.

Thank you for giving me peace, Lord, even during these present circumstances. Let my cry come before you, O Lord. Give me understanding according to your Word. Let my supplication come before you. My lips shall utter praise to you.

Thank you, Father, for being with me during this time of affliction, and for hearing and answering my prayer. I love you with all my heart.

In Jesus' name I pray, Amen.

Scriptures: Psalm 25; Psalm 106; Psalm 119.

Personal Affirmation: I will get through this time of affliction realizing that God is with me and that He loves me with an everlasting love. He knows what I am going through and He is helping me.

New Testament Scripture: "For our light affliction,

which is but for a moment, worketh for us a far more exceeding and eternal weight of glory; while we look not at the things which are seen: for the things which are seen are temporal; but the things which are not seen are eternal" (2 Corinthians 4:17-18).

Reflection: *"Though we are incomplete, God loves us completely. Though we are imperfect, He loves us perfectly. Though we may feel lost and without compass, God's love encompasses us completely. . . . He loves every one of us, even those who are flawed, rejected, awkward, sorrowful, or broken"* (Dieter F. Uchtdorf).

3
ANGELS—GOD'S AMBASSADORS

The angel of the Lord encampeth round about
them that fear him, and delivereth them.
(Psalm 34:7)

Central Truth: Angels are watching over you every minute of every day.

Central Focus: Angels are God's ministering spirits, and they encamp around us to help us and deliver us from evil. I thank God for the angelic protection He gives to me.

Prayer: Father, thank you for sending angels to be with me. I know that they are ministering to me even as I pray. I will bless you at all times and I will continually praise you. My soul will make its boast in you, Lord God. When I sought you, Lord, you rescued me, and you delivered me from all my fears. Hallelujah!

When I look unto you, your light shines upon me, and my face is not ashamed. Thank you for your angelic protection in my life. Let your angels encamp around me and my family.

Your chariots are 20,000 in number, and there are thousands of angels. Thank you for being among them, Father. Blessed are you, dear Lord, for you daily load me with benefits. Praise your name!

It gives me a sense of great security, Lord God, to know that you have given your angels charge over me, to keep me in all my ways. They shall bear me up in their hands, lest I dash my foot against a stone. Thank you, God.

Thank you, Father God, for preparing your throne in the heavens. Your kingdom rules over everything. Hallelujah! Your angels excel in strength, and I thank you that they are surrounding me and doing your commandments. Indeed, they hearken unto the voice of your Word.

As I pray your Word, Father, I know the angels are surrounding me. Bless you, O Lord, for you are very great. You are clothed with glory and majesty. You cover yourself with light as with a garment. You stretch out the heavens like a curtain. You lay the beams of your chambers in the waters. You make the clouds your chariot, and you walk upon the wings of the wind.

Thank you for making your angels become ministering spirits to me. Truly, they are like a flaming fire. I join with the angels in praising you, Father. I praise your mighty name, for your name is excellent. Your glory is above the earth and heaven.

Let your angels do their work in my midst, Father, and may I never forget that they are always with me.

In the mighty name of Jesus I pray, Amen.

Scriptures: Psalm 34; Psalm 68; Psalm 91; Psalm 103; Psalm 104; Psalm 148.

Personal Affirmation: I praise God for His ministering spirits, the angels, and I rejoice that they are protecting me. They will keep me from all evil. I will trust God to send His angels to my defense whenever I need them.

New Testament Scripture: "And of the angels he saith, Who maketh his angels spirits, and his ministers a flame of fire" (Hebrews 1:7).

Reflection: *"Legalism says God will love us if we change. The gospel says God will change us because He loves us"* (Tullian Tchividjian).

4
BLESSEDNESS—YOUR PERPETUAL STATE OF BEING

Blessed is the man that walketh not in the counsel of the ungodly, nor standeth in the way of sinners, nor sitteth in the seat of the scornful.
But his delight is in the law of the Lord; and in his law doth he meditate day and night.
(Psalm 1:1-2)

Central Truth: The state of blessedness, which is rightfully yours as a child of God, is a state of true happiness and joy that can be found only in Him.

Central Focus: To be blessed is to be happy in the Lord. It comes from knowing God, His Word, and His ways and following them. God wants you to be blessed.

Prayer: Help me, Father, to remember never to walk in the counsel of the ungodly and never to stand in the way of sinners or sit in the seat of the scornful. Thank you for your Word, which gives great delight and blessedness to me. I will meditate in your Word both night and day.

Thank you for your promise that I will be like a tree that is planted by the rivers of water and brings forth its fruit in the right season. I believe your Word, which tells me that my leaf will not wither and whatever I do shall prosper. It is my desire, Lord, to be a fruitful believer all the time.

I place all my trust in you, Father, and, as I do so, I realize that this is the source of blessedness in my life. Thank you for blessing me in so many ways. I rejoice in the blessedness you've given to me. Truly, you have made me most blessed forever, and you have made me exceedingly glad with your countenance.

Lord, you are my trust. Many are your wonderful works. I delight to do your will, O my God. Your Word is within my heart. I have preached your righteousness in the great congregation. I have not restrained my lips, O Lord.

Thank you for all you are doing in my life, Lord. Thank you for choosing me and permitting me to approach you and to dwell in your courts. I shall be ever satisfied with the goodness of your house. Thank you for letting me hear the joyful sound and for permitting me, O Lord, to walk in the light of your countenance.

Thank you for chastening me, Father, and for teaching me the truths of your Word. Thank you for giving me rest from all adversity. I praise you, Lord, and I greatly respect you, as I delight in your commandments.

Help me to remain undefiled in the way and to walk in your Word. Help me to keep your testimonies and to seek you with all my heart. I choose to walk in your ways, Father, and to honor your name.

In the blessed name of Jesus I pray, Amen.

Scriptures: Psalm 1; Psalm 2; Psalm 21; Psalm 40; Psalm 65; Psalm 89; Psalm 94; Psalm 112; Psalm 119; Psalm 128.

Personal Affirmation: I will count my blessings as I go throughout each day. By so doing I will realize that God has placed me in a state of blessedness. I will bless the Lord for His goodness to me.

New Testament Scripture: "Blessed are the poor in spirit: for theirs is the kingdom of heaven. Blessed are they that mourn: for they shall be comforted. Blessed are the meek: for they shall inherit the earth. Blessed are they which do hunger and thirst after righteousness: for they shall be filled. Blessed are the merciful: for they shall obtain mercy. Blessed are the pure in heart: for they shall see God. Blessed are the peacemakers: for they shall be called the children of God. Blessed are they which are persecuted for righteousness' sake: for theirs is the kingdom of heaven. Blessed are ye, when men shall revile you, and persecute you, and shall say all manner of evil against you for my sake" (Matthew 5:3-11).

Reflection: *"Too much of anything is dangerous unless it's God's love"* (Reign).

5

BURDENS—THE LORD IS YOUR BURDEN-BEARER

Cast thy burden upon the Lord, and he shall sustain thee: he shall never suffer the righteous to be moved.
(Psalm 55:22)

Central Truth: Carrying the cross makes all burdens lighter. Jesus' yoke is easy and His burden is light. (See Matthew 11:30.)

Central Focus: God is the great burden-bearer. Jesus, who loved the Psalms, said, "Come unto me, all ye that labour and are heavy laden, and I will give you rest. Take my yoke upon you, and learn of me; for I am meek and lowly in heart: and ye shall find rest unto your souls. For my yoke is easy, and my burden is light" (Matthew 11:28–30). God will sustain me as I learn to cast my burdens upon Him.

Prayer: Abba-Father, I cast my burdens upon you, and I thank you for your promise to sustain me and give me your rest. Give ear to my prayer, O God, and hide not yourself from my supplication. Attend to me, and hear me. I call upon you, and I know you will help me. You will bear my burdens with me. Thank you so much.

My iniquities are a heavy burden. Thank you for lifting them from me as I confess them to you. In you, O

Lord, do I hope, because I know you hear my prayers. Hallelujah! Forsake me not, O Lord, and be not far from me. Make haste to help me, O God of my salvation.

I call to you, Father, and I know you will deliver me from this burden. Thank you for answering me in the secret place of thunder. I hearken unto you as I pray. Thank you for satisfying me with honey from the rock.

As I wait for you, Lord, you are inclining unto me and hearing my cry. Thank you for bringing me up out of a horrible pit and out of the miry clay. Thank you for setting my feet upon a rock and establishing my goings. Thank you for putting a new song in my mouth, even praise unto you, O Most High!

I am greatly blessed, Father, because I have made you my trust. Many, O God, are your wonderful works. I delight to do your will. Your Word is within my heart. I have not hid your righteousness within my heart. I have declared your faithfulness and your salvation. I have not concealed your loving-kindness and your truth from the great congregation.

Let your loving-kindness and your truth continually preserve me and take my burdens from me. Be pleased, O Lord, to deliver me. O Lord, make haste to help me. Instead of focusing on my burdens, I will rejoice and be glad in you. May you and your name be magnified.

Thank you for lifting my burdens from me and giving me your wonderful peace.

In the Savior's name I pray, Amen.

Scriptures: Psalm 55, Psalm 38; Psalm 81; Psalm 40.

Personal Affirmation: The mighty God is lifting all my burdens from me as I learn to trust in Him. In Him I have discovered true rest for my soul.

New Testament Scripture: "Come unto me, all ye that labour and are heavy laden, and I will give you rest. Take my yoke upon you, and learn of me; for I am meek and lowly in heart: and ye shall find rest for your souls. For my yoke is easy, and my burden is light" (Matthew 11:28–30).

Reflection: *"We obey God's law, not to be loved, but because we are loved in Christ"* (Jerry Bridges).

6
COMFORT—THE HOLY SPIRIT IS YOUR COMFORTER

Thy rod and thy staff they comfort me.
(Psalm 23:4)

Central Truth: God is the God of all comfort. Let Him bring comfort, peace, and rest to your soul.

Central Focus: The Holy Spirit is my Comforter, and my Father is the God of all comfort. Comfort comes to me when I linger in His presence. He loves me with an everlasting love.

Prayer: Heavenly Father, I come to you now to receive the comfort I need. You are my Shepherd, and I shall not want. You make me lie down in green pastures, and you lead me beside the still waters. Thank you for restoring my soul and leading me in the paths of righteousness for your name's sake. Even when I walk through the valley of the shadow of death, I will fear no evil, for you are with me. Your rod and your staff bring great comfort to me. Thank you, Father.

Your righteousness, O Lord, is very high, and you have done great and mighty things. There is no one like you. Quicken me again and bring me up from the depths. Let your comforting presence minister unto me. I ask you to comfort me on every side, and I know you will through your grace and mercy.

A source of great comfort to me, Father, is the knowledge that your Word quickens me. Thank you for your Word, which is a lamp unto my feet and a light unto my path. Let your tender mercies come unto me, that I may live, for your Word is my delight.

I find great hope in your Word, Father. In your Word I find the comfort I need. Forever, O Lord, your Word is settled in Heaven, and your faithfulness is to all generations. Thank you so much for your Word and your faithfulness.

O, how I love your Word. It is my meditation all the day, and this I find great comfort. Thank you, Father.

In the name of your Son, the Lord Jesus, I pray, Amen.

Scriptures: Psalm 23; Psalm 71; Psalm 119.

Personal Affirmation: I am comforted as I pray and meditate upon God's Word. This lifts me out of any discouragement and grief I may be experiencing. My heart will be filled with gratitude for God's comforting presence in my life.

New Testament Scripture: "Blessed be God, even the Father of our Lord Jesus Christ, the Father of mercies, and the God of all comfort; who comforteth us in all our tribulation, that we may be able to comfort them which are in any trouble, by the comfort wherewith we ourselves are comforted of God" (2 Corinthians 1:3-4).

Reflection: *"Here's the paradox. We can fully embrace*

God's love only when we recognize how completely unworthy of it we are" (Ann Tatlock).

7
COMMITMENT—HOLDING FAST THROUGH EVERYTHING

Commit thy way unto the Lord;
and he will bring it to pass.
(Psalm 37:5)

Central Truth: Commitment is the key to a victorious Christian life. Commit your way to the Lord, and He will direct your steps. (See Psalm 37:5.)

Central Focus: I have committed my life to Jesus Christ. He is my Lord and Savior. I now belong to Him. Everything I am and have belongs to Him.

Prayer: Lord God, I trust in you. Help me always to do good and to dwell in the land you've given to me. Through your grace I will delight myself in you, and I know you will give me the desires of my heart. Thank you, Father.

As I commit my way unto you and trust completely in you, I know you will bring good things to pass in my life. As I rest in you and wait patiently upon you, I will not worry about evildoers who seem to prosper. Help me to cease from anger and forsake wrath.

In a little while the wicked will no longer be. Praise your name, Lord, for your promise that the meek will inherit the earth and shall delight themselves in the abundance of peace. With your help I will walk in meekness.

Thank you for showing me that what a righteous person has is better than the riches of many wicked people. Thank you for upholding me, Father, and for giving me an everlasting inheritance. It is so good to know that my steps are ordered by you and that I shall not be utterly cast down even when I fall, because you, dear Lord, always uphold me with your hand.

I have been young and now I am older, but I have never seen your righteous children begging for bread. Praise you, Father. Therefore, I will depart from evil and do good. Thank you for your promise that I will live forevermore.

Help me to use my mouth and tongue to speak only wisdom. Help me to keep your Word within my heart. May none of my steps ever slide. I will wait on you, Lord, and I know you will exalt me. Praise your mighty name!

In the sacred name of Jesus I pray, Amen.

Scriptures: Psalm 37.

Personal Affirmation: I commit everything I am and have to the Lord, knowing that He loves me with an everlasting love.

New Testament Scripture: "Keep that which is committed to thy trust, avoiding profane and vain babblings, and oppositions of science falsely so called: which some professing have erred concerning the faith" (1 Timothy 6:20-21).

Reflection: *"That is why He warned people to 'count the cost' before becoming Christians. 'Make no mistake,' He says, 'if you let me, I will make you perfect. The moment you put yourself in my hands, that is what you are in for. Nothing less, or other than that"* (C.S. Lewis).

8
DELIGHT—BEING IN THE LORD'S PRESENCE

Thou wilt shew me the path of life: in thy presence is fulness of joy; at thy right hand there are pleasures for evermore.
(Psalm 16:11)

Central Truth: The greatest source of delight in life comes from an intimate relationship with the Lord. Nothing can be compared to the delight this brings to your heart.

Central Focus: I find my delight in God and His Word. I will walk in His Word and enjoy the blessings He showers upon me. I delight to do His will and to follow Him every step of my way.

Prayer: O God, my Lord, I will trust in you at all times and delight myself in you. You are my delight and my joy. Thank you for the promise that the meek shall inherit the Earth. I will delight myself in the abundance of peace you give to me.

I delight to do your will, O my God. Your Word is a treasure within my heart. Your comforts bring delight to my soul, O Lord. I take great delight in your statutes, Father, and your testimonies are my delight. Help me to walk in your commandments, for as I do so, I experience great delight. I love your commandments, Father.

Your Word delights me. Let your tender mercies come to me, that I may live. Your Word will always be the delight of my life. Let my cry come before you, O Lord. Give me understanding according to your Word. Let my supplication come before you, and deliver me according to your Word.

My lips shall utter praise, and my tongue will speak of your Word, for I know that all your commandments are righteousness. Let your hand help me, for I have chosen your precepts. I have longed for your salvation, O Lord, and your Word is my delight.

Praise the name of the Lord!

In Jesus' name I pray and take my delight, Amen.

Scriptures: Psalm 34; Psalm 37; Psalm 40; Psalm 94; Psalm 119; Psalm 139.

Personal Affirmation: I will delight myself in God and His Word. His Word will always be my delight. I am filled with joy as I contemplate everything He has done for me.

New Testament Scripture: "For I delight in the law of God after the inward man" (Romans 7:22).

Reflection: *"We have one function in life: to be the manifestors of His life to the world. Only when we are living His life are we truly living our own! This is the reason for our creation"* (Malcolm Smith).

9

DELIVERANCE—THE LORD IS YOUR DELIVERER

*I will love thee, O Lord, my strength. The Lord is my
rock, and my fortress, and my deliverer; my God,
my strength, in whom I will trust; my buckler, and
the horn of my salvation, and my high tower.*
(Psalm 18:1-2)

Central Truth: God delivers His people from every form
of evil, including addictions, sin, and hardships. He is
mighty to deliver you!

Central Focus: God is my Deliverer. He gives me great
security. In Him I find peace and rest. Deliverance from
evil, sin, and hardships comes from Him alone.

Prayer: I will love you, O Lord, my strength. You are my
rock, my fortress, and my Deliverer. You are my God
and my strength, and I will trust in you. You are my
buckler, the horn of my salvation, and my high tower.
Thank you for bringing deliverance to me.

I will call upon you, O Lord, and in doing so I will be
saved from my enemies. Praise your holy name! Thank
you for delivering me from my strong enemy and from
all who hated me. Thank you for bringing me into a
large place and delivering me. It thrills me to know that
you delight in me, Father.

You will light my candle, Lord, and enlighten my

darkness. By you I have run through a troop and I have leaped over a wall. Your way is perfect, my Father, and your Word is tried. Thank you for being my buckler as I learn to trust in you.

Help me to remember that a mighty man is not delivered by much strength and a horse is a vain thing for safety. Thank you for keeping your eye upon me, Father, as I hope in your mercy. Thank you for delivering my soul from death. My heart shall rejoice in you, and I will trust in your holy name forever.

I will bless you at all times, O Lord, and your praise shall continually be in my mouth. My soul will make its boast in you. I thank you that you heard me when I sought you, and you delivered me from all my fears. You are my helper, O God. Give ear to the words of my mouth.

I will freely sacrifice unto you and praise your holy name, O Lord, for it is good. Thank you for delivering me out of all trouble. I give thanks to you, Father, for you are good. Your mercy endures forever. Hallelujah! Thank you for redeeming me from the hand of the enemy. I praise you for your goodness and for your wonderful works.

Thank you for satisfying my longing soul and filling my hungry soul with goodness. Thank you for bringing me out of darkness and the shadow of death.

In the name of my Deliverer I pray, Amen.

Scriptures: Psalm 18; Psalm 33; Psalm 34; Psalm 54.

Personal Affirmation: God is my deliverer, and I will let others know about Him and His delivering power. I will walk in His deliverance every day of my life.

New Testament Scripture: "The Lord knoweth how to deliver the godly out of temptations" (2 Peter 2:9).

Reflection: *"The Lord never came to deliver men from the consequences of their sins while yet those sins remained. . . . Yet men, loving their sins and feeling nothing of their dread hatefulness, have, consistent with their low condition, constantly taken this word concerning the Lord to mean that He came to save them from the punishment of their sins"* (George MacDonald).

10
DESIRES—GOD WILL GRANT YOU THE DESIRES OF YOUR HEART

Delight thyself also in the Lord; and he shall give thee the desires of thine heart.
(Psalm 37:4)

Central Truth: As you learn to let your desires line up with the Word of God, they will be fulfilled. God desires to meet your needs and to give you the desires of your heart.

Central Focus: The desire of my heart is fulfilled in Jesus. I desire what He desires, I want what He wants, and I will live for Him forever. I want the desires of my heart to match up with His. Then I know He will grant me the desires of my heart.

Prayer: God, I delight in you, and I am so thankful for your promise that you will give me the desires of my heart. Praise your holy name!

Lord, all my desire is before you, and my groaning is not hid from you. In you do I hope, for I know you will hear me, O God. It is wonderful to know that you are continually with me, Father, and you have held me up by your right hand. Hallelujah!

I know you will guide me with your counsel, and afterward you will receive me into glory. Who do I have in Heaven besides you? There is no one on Earth that I desire more than you. You are the strength of my heart and my portion forever.

Thank you for always being on my side, Father. I will not fear. What can man do to me? Let me see my desire fulfilled upon those who hate me. I know it is better to trust in you than it is to put confidence in human beings. I trust in you, Lord.

You are my strength and my song, and you are my salvation. Hallelujah! I will declare your works as long as I live. Open to me the gates of righteousness and I will go through them and praise your name. Thank you for hearing my prayer.

Your doings are marvelous in my eyes, Father. This is the day you have made, and I will rejoice and be glad in it. I will ever praise you, for you are the desire of my heart.

Your kingdom is an everlasting kingdom and your dominion endures throughout all generations. You uphold all who fall and you raise up all those who are bowed down. Thank you, Father. I wait upon you. Thank you for opening your hand and satisfying the desires of all who come to you.

It is so wonderful to know that you are near to all that call upon you in truth. I know you will fulfill my desires, Father, and I know you will hear my cry. Thank you for preserving me. My mouth shall speak praises unto you, and I will bless your holy name forever.

Thank you, Father, for granting the desires of my heart.

In Jesus' name I pray, Amen.

Scriptures: Psalm 37; Psalm 38; Psalm 73; Psalm 118; Psalm 145.

Personal Affirmation: As I meditate upon God's Word, my mind will be renewed in such a way that God's desires will become my desires. I will desire what God wants for me, as I walk with Him each step of the way.

New Testament Scripture: "Therefore I say unto you, what things soever ye desire, when ye pray, believe that ye receive them, and ye shall have them" (Mark 11:24).

Reflection: *"To abandon all, to strip one's self of all, in order to seek and follow Jesus Christ naked to Bethlehem where He was born, naked to the hall where He was scourged, and naked to Calvary where He died on the cross, is so great a mercy that neither the thing nor the knowledge of it, is given to any but through faith in the Son of God"* (John Wesley).

11

EVERLASTING LIFE—
YOUR GIFT FROM GOD

Lord, thou hast been our dwelling place in all generations. Before the mountains were brought forth, or ever thou hadst formed the earth and the world, even from everlasting to everlasting, thou art God.
(Psalm 90:1-2)

Central Truth: God gives eternal life to all who come to Him by faith in His Son, the Lord Jesus Christ. What a wonderful gift this is.

Central Focus: God has given us everlasting life through His Son, the Lord Jesus Christ. This is a life that will never end. "For God so loved the world, that he gave his only begotten Son, that whosoever believeth in him should not perish, but have everlasting life" (John 3:16).

Prayer: Lord, you have been our dwelling place in all generations. Before the mountains were brought forth, or ever thou hadst formed the earth and the world, even from everlasting to everlasting, you are God. I love you with all my heart, soul, and strength.

Thank you, Father, for imparting everlasting life to me. I will make a joyful noise to you, Lord God, and serve you with gladness. I come before your presence with thanksgiving. You are my God; I am a sheep in your pasture. I will enter your gates with thanksgiving and go into your courts with praise. I will ever be thankful to you and bless your name.

You are so good, Lord, and your mercy is everlasting. I praise you that your truth will endure to all generations. I bless you, O Lord; all that is within me blesses your holy name. I will never forget all your benefits to me. Thank you for forgiving all my iniquities and healing all my diseases. Thank you for redeeming my life from destruction and crowning me with your tender mercies.

You have satisfied my mouth with good things, and you have renewed my youth like the eagle's. I thank you for your mercy, which is from everlasting to everlasting. Help me to keep your covenant and remember to do your commandments. Thank you for the everlasting covenant that you have given to your children.

O Lord, you have searched me and known me. You know when I sit down and when I rise up. You understand my thoughts from afar. You know every word I speak. I will praise you, for I am fearfully and wonderfully made. Marvelous are all your works.

Search me, O God, and know my heart: try me, and know my thoughts, and see if there be any wicked way in me, and lead me in the way everlasting. Surely goodness and mercy shall follow me, and I will dwell in your house forever. Praise your mighty name.

Thank you for everlasting life.

In Jesus' name I pray, Amen.

Scriptures: Psalm 90; Psalm 100; Psalm 103; Psalm 139; Psalm 23.

Personal Affirmation: God has given eternal life to me. Praise His mighty name. I look forward to the time when I will be with Him forever.

New Testament Scripture: "For the wages of sin is death; but the gift of God is eternal life through Jesus Christ our Lord" (Romans 6:23).

Reflection: *"The life Christ lived qualified Him for the death He died—and the death He died qualifies us for the life we live"* (Unknown).

12
EVIL—AVOIDING EVIL AND THE EVIL ONE

Depart from evil, and do good; and dwell forevermore.
(Psalm 37:27)

Central Truth: Evil is at work in the world, and the only way to counteract it is through faith in the Lord Jesus Christ in whom there is no evil or guile.

Central Focus: Whenever I am aware of evil, I will expose it, walk away from it, and warn others about it. God promises to deliver me from all evil.

Prayer: O God my Father, I come to you now in the name of Jesus, and I am thankful that you are not a God that takes pleasure in wickedness. Evil will never dwell with you. As for me, I will come into your house through your mercy, and I will worship toward your holy temple. Lead me, O Lord, in your righteousness.

I will fear no evil, for I know you are with me. Thank you, Father. Help me to keep my tongue from evil and my lips from ever speaking guile. Through your grace I will always depart from evil and do good. I will seek and pursue peace.

I am learning to rest in you, O Lord, as I wait patiently upon you. I will not worry about those who seem to prosper even though they are evil. Help me to cease from anger and to forsake wrath.

O satisfy me early with your mercy, that I may rejoice and be glad all my days. Make me glad, Father, and establish the work of my hands. I praise you for your promise that no evil will befall me. I believe this and claim it for me and my family, Father. I know you will give your angels charge over me, to keep me in all my ways. Praise your holy name.

You, O Lord, are high above all the Earth. You are exalted far above all gods. I love you, and I hate evil. Thank you for preserving my soul and delivering me out of the hands of the wicked. I highly respect you, my Father, and I delight greatly in all your commandments. I will not be afraid of evil tidings, because my heart is fixed, as I trust in you.

I have refrained my feet from every evil way, that I might keep your Word. Hallelujah! I lift up my eyes to the hills from whence my help comes. My help comes from you, O Lord. I know you will not permit my foot to be moved and that you never slumber nor sleep.

You are my keeper, O Lord, and you are the shade upon my right hand. The sun will not smite me by day, and the moon shall not smite me by night. You, O Lord, will preserve me from all evil. You will preserve my soul. Thank you, Lord, for your promise to preserve my going out and my coming in from this day forward.

Deliver me, O Lord, from evil people. Preserve me from the violent. Keep me, O Lord, from the hands of the wicked. You are my God. Hear the voice of my supplications.

In the good name of Jesus I pray, Amen.

Scriptures: Psalm 5; Psalm 23; Psalm 34; Psalm 37; Psalm 90; Psalm 91; Psalm 97; Psalm 112; Psalm 119; Psalm 121; Psalm 140.

Personal Affirmation: With God's help I will turn away from all evil. I will expose evildoers. I will walk in the righteousness of God from this day forward.

New Testament Scripture: "Be not overcome of evil, but overcome evil with good" (Romans 12:21).

Reflection: *"If I obey Jesus Christ in the seemingly random circumstances of life, they become pinholes through which I see the face of God"* (Oswald Chambers).

13
FEAR—NO NEED TO FEAR ANYONE OR ANYTHING

The Lord is my light and my salvation; whom shall I fear? The Lord is the strength of my life; of whom shall I be afraid?
(Psalm 27:1)

Central Truth: There is no fear in God's love. Remember it His good pleasure to give you His kingdom, which consists of righteousness, peace, and joy in the Holy Spirit.

Central Focus: Love is the perfect antidote for fear, and faith dispels all fear from my life. Therefore, I place all my faith and trust in God, and I know He will eradicate all fear from my life.

Prayer: Father–God, I thank you for all the promises of your Word. You are my light and my salvation. Whom shall I fear? You are the strength of my life. In light of these truths, of whom shall I be afraid? Though a host of enemies would encamp against me, my heart shall not fear, for in the time of trouble I know you will hide me in your pavilion. You will set me upon a rock. Hallelujah!

You are my refuge and my strength, dear Father. You are a very present help in trouble. Therefore, I will not fear. Thank you for always being with me. I will be still and know that you are God. You will be exalted among the heathen. You will be exalted in the Earth. Praise your mighty name!

Be merciful to me, O God. Whenever I am tempted to be afraid, I will trust in you and I will praise your Word. I will never fear what others can do to me. I place all my trust in you, Father, and I will not be afraid of others, for you have delivered my soul from death and my feet from falling, that I may walk before you in the light of the living. Praise the Lord!

Hear my voice, O God, in my prayer, and preserve my life from fear of the enemy. I shall be glad in you, Lord God, and I shall trust in you. You are on my side, O Lord; therefore, I will not fear. What can man do to me?

It is so much better to put my trust in you than to put confidence in human beings. I trust you completely, Father. You are my strength and my song. I will praise you, for you have heard me. You are my God, and I will exalt you and I give thanks to you, for you are good and your mercy endures forever.

Thank you for delivering me from all fear, Father.

In the mighty name of Jesus I pray, Amen.

Scriptures: Psalm 27; Psalm 46; Psalm 56; Psalm 64; Psalm 118.

Personal Affirmation: Instead of being afraid and living in fear, I will trust in the name of the Lord who always keeps me safe. Through His grace I will overcome all fear.

New Testament Scripture: "There is no fear in love; but perfect love casteth out fear: because fear hath torment. He that feareth is not made perfect in love" (1 John 4:18).

Reflection: *"Four things let us ever keep in mind: God hears prayer, God heeds prayer, God answers prayer, and God delivers by prayer"* (E.M. Bounds).

14

GLADNESS—THE ATTITUDE OF A SERVANT

Thou hast put gladness in my heart, more than in the time that their corn and their wine increased.
(Psalm 4:7)

Central Truth: Gladness involves pleasure and joy at the deepest levels. God's gladness makes you happy and very willing to please Him.

Central Focus: The joy of the Lord is my strength (see Nehemiah 8:10), and He makes me glad. I will walk in His gladness today and always.

Prayer: Father, thank you for putting gladness in my heart. Hear, O Lord, and have mercy upon me. Be my helper. Thank you for turning my mourning into dancing for me and taking off my sackcloth. I rejoice in the truth that you have girded me with gladness, Father, to the end that my glory may sing praise to you and not be silent. O Lord my God, I will give thanks to you forever.

Thank you for anointing me with gladness. Make me to hear joy and gladness, Father. Hide your face from my sins and blot out all my iniquities. Create in me a clean spirit, O God, and renew a right spirit within me. Cast me not away from your presence, and do not take your Holy Spirit from me. Restore unto me the joy of your salvation, and uphold me with your free spirit.

O Lord, open my lips, and my mouth will show forth your praise. Hallelujah! You, O Lord, are high above all the Earth, and you are exalted far above all gods. I love you, Father, and I hate evil. Thank you for preserving my soul and delivering me from the wicked. I rejoice in you and I give thanks, as I remember your holiness.

I make a joyful noise unto you, O Lord. I serve you with gladness and come before your presence with singing. I know that you, Lord, are God. You made me. I am a sheep in your pasture, and the knowledge of this makes me glad. I enter your gates with thanksgiving and go into your courts with praise. I am thankful to you and I praise your holy name, for you are good and your mercy is everlasting. Your truth endures to all generations.

Thank you for bringing me forth with gladness and joy. I will praise you, O Lord, with my whole heart; I will show forth all your marvelous works. I will be glad and rejoice in you. I have set you always before my face. You are at my right hand, and I shall never be moved. Therefore, my heart is glad and my glory rejoices. I rest in the hope you have imparted to me.

Thank you for showing me the path of life. In your presence there is fullness of joy; at your right hand there are pleasures forevermore. Praise your holy name, Father! I will be glad in you and rejoice. I will shout for joy!

Thank you for giving me so much gladness, Lord.

In the name of Jesus I pray, Amen.

Scriptures: Psalm 4; Psalm 30; Psalm 45; Psalm 51; Psalm 97; Psalm 100; Psalm 105; Psalm 9; Psalm 16; Psalm 32.

Personal Affirmation: God has filled my heart with gladness. I will be glad and rejoice in Him from this time forth. He is helping me walk in gladness every day of my life.

New Testament Scripture: "Thou hast loved righteousness, and hated iniquity; therefore God, even thy God, hath anointed thee with the oil of gladness above thy fellows" (Hebrews 1:9).

Reflection: *"There is not in the world a kind of life more sweet and delightful than that of a continual conversation with God"* (Brother Lawrence).

15
HELP—YOUR HELP IS IN THE NAME OF THE LORD

Our soul waiteth for the Lord; he is our help and our shield.
(Psalm 33:20)

Central Truth: God will never let you down. His promise to help you will always be active. Praise His holy name!

Central Focus: God is my help. I will go to Him whenever I need help. He is faithful, and He will never let me down.

Prayer: Be not far from me, O Lord. O my strength, hasten to help me. You are my help. Do not leave me nor forsake me, O God of my salvation. My soul waits for you, O Lord, for you are my help and my shield. Hallelujah! My heart will rejoice in you and I will trust your holy name. Let your mercy be upon me, as I hope in you.

Forsake me not, O Lord. O my God, don't be far from me. Make haste to help me, O Lord of my salvation. Thank you for being my help and my Deliverer. God, you are my refuge and strength, a very present help in times of trouble. Thank you, Father, for the help you always provide for me.

Because your loving-kindness is better than life to me, my lips shall praise you. Thus will I bless you while I live. I will lift up my hands in your name. All my help comes from you, Lord God, and I know you will not permit my foot to be moved. I am thankful that you will not slumber nor sleep. You are my Keeper, Lord God, and you are my shade upon my right hand. Thank you for your promise that you will preserve my coming in and my going out forever.

My help is in your name, O Lord. Hear, O Lord, and have mercy upon me, for you are my Helper. Thank you, Father. I thank you for being my helper, and for always being with me. Thank you for delivering me out of all trouble.

I hope in you, my Father. I will praise you for the help of your countenance. Thank you for commanding your loving-kindness to come unto me. I will keep hoping in you, for you are the health of my countenance, and you are my God.

Give me your help from all trouble, Father, for I know the help of others is vain. I need your help. Through you I shall do valiantly, for you will tread down all my enemies. Praise your holy name!

Help me, O Lord my God. Save me according to your mercy. May others know that it was your hand that helped me, and that you, Lord, accomplished this for me.

Thank you for always being there to help me, Father.

In the prevailing name of Jesus I pray, Amen.

Scriptures: Psalm 22; Psalm 27; Psalm 33; Psalm 38; Psalm 40; Psalm 46; Psalm 63; Psalm 121; Psalm 124; Psalm 30; Psalm 54; Psalm 42; Psalm 109.

Personal Affirmation: I trust God to help me in every situation. I know He will see me through. Therefore, I place all my hope, trust, and confidence in Him.

New Testament Scripture: "Let us therefore come boldly unto the throne of grace, that we may obtain mercy, and find grace to help in time of need" (Hebrews 4:16).

Reflection: *"Praying in faith is not an inner conviction that God will act according to our desires if only we believe hard enough. It involves believing that God will always respond to our prayers in accord with His nature, His purposes, and His promises"* (Alvin VanderGriend).

16
HOPE—THE GOD OF ALL HOPE IS WITH YOU

For in thee, O Lord, do I hope: thou wilt hear,
O Lord my God.
(Psalm 38:15)

Central Truth: Hope is the anchor for your soul. As you hope in God, you will never drift again. Hope in God, for He is everything to you.

Central Focus: I hope in God, for He is my rock, my fortress, and my Deliverer. The hope He imparts to me is an anchor for my soul.

Prayer: O God, my hope, I bless you. Thank you for giving me counsel from your Word. I have set you always before me. Because you are at my right hand, I shall never be moved. Therefore, my heart is glad and my glory rejoices. My flesh shall always rest in the hope you've given to me. Thank you, Father.

Oh, how great is your goodness, Father, which you have laid up for me and wrought for me. Hide me in the secret of your presence. Blessed be your name, O Lord. Thank you for revealing your kindness to me. I love you and I will be of good courage, for I know you are strengthening my heart, as I hope in you.

I thank you, Father, for letting me know that your eye is upon me, as I hope in your mercy. You will deliver my soul from death. Hallelujah! My soul waits for you, for you are my help and my shield. My heart rejoices in you, as I trust in you. Let your mercy, O Lord, be upon me, according as I hope in you.

I put all my hope in you, Lord, and I know you will hear me as I pray. I will ever hope in you, Father, and I will praise you, for you are the help of my countenance. Praise your holy name! I will hope continually in you, and I will praise you more and more.

Thank you for your mighty Word, which causes me to hope in you. I find hope in your Word, Father. I wait for you, O Lord, and in your Word I hope. I know that with you there is mercy and plenteous redemption. Thank you, Father.

You make me happy, Lord, for you are my help, and all my hope is in you. Thank you for taking pleasure in me, Father, as I learn to hope in you. I trust completely in your Word, Father, and I hope in your judgments. I hope in your Word, which is a lamp unto my feet and a lamp unto my path.

Praise you for the hope you have imparted unto me, Lord God.

In the name of Jesus I pray, Amen.

Scriptures: Psalm 16; Psalm 31; Psalm 33; Psalm 38; Psalm 42; Psalm 71; Psalm 119; Psalm 130; Psalm 146; Psalm 147; Psalm 119.

Personal Affirmation: Because I know Jesus as my

personal Savior, I know that I will never experience any feelings of hopelessness or helplessness again. The God of all hope fills me with hope, and I will walk in the hope He imparts each and every day of my life.

New Testament Scripture: "To whom God would make known what is the riches of the glory of this mystery among the Gentiles; which is Christ in you, the hope of glory" (Colossians 1:27).

Reflection: *"In Christ, troubles are turned into triumph, so in Him we look at what is coming as the times of the greatest triumphs the world has ever known! The conclusion of all things is that we win! The cross will prevail. This is the foundational truth that all of our understanding of these times must be based upon"* (Rick Joyner).

17
INHERITANCE—IN CHRIST YOU HAVE EVERYTHING YOU NEED

The Lord is the portion of my inheritance and of my cup: thou maintainest my lot.
(Psalm 16:5)

Central Truth: You are an heir of God, and a joint-heir with His Son, Jesus Christ, in whom you have inherited all things pertaining to godliness.

Central Focus: God has blessed me with every spiritual blessing in Christ Jesus. (See Ephesians 1:3.) I am a joint heir with Jesus. In Him I've inherited all things.

Prayer: O God, I thank you for the inheritance you've imparted unto me. You are my strength and my shield. My heart trusts in you and I rejoice. With my song I will praise you. Thank you for being my saving strength. Bless your inheritance, Father, and lift me up as I pray.

Thank you for choosing me to be your inheritance. Hallelujah! Thank you for your promise that my inheritance will go on forever. Thank you for choosing my inheritance for me. I know you will never cast me off nor forsake me.

My soul shall dwell at ease, and I know I shall inherit the Earth. I thank you that your secret is with me and you are showing me your covenant. My eyes are ever toward you, Lord. Turn unto me and have mercy upon me.

Help me to be a meek person, Father, for I know the meek shall inherit the Earth and I shall delight in the abundance of peace you've provided for me as a part of my inheritance. Praise your name, mighty God.

Order my steps, Lord, for I delight in your way. Thank you for upholding me with your hand. Through your grace I will depart from evil and do good. In so doing I know I will live forevermore with you. Hallelujah!

I wait on you, O Lord, and I will keep your way. Thank you for your promise to exalt me so that I would inherit the land. Thank you for all your promises. I know you will enable me to inherit your blessings, because I love your name.

Thank you so much for blessing me with your inheritance.

In Jesus' name, Amen.

Scriptures: Psalm 28; Psalm 33; Psalm 37; Psalm 47; Psalm 94; Psalm 25; Psalm 37; Psalm 69.

Personal Affirmation: God has blessed me so abundantly. I am His inheritance, and He is mine. I will enjoy the blessings He has poured out on me every day.

New Testament Scripture: "And if children, then heirs; heirs of God, and joint-heirs with Christ; if so be that we suffer with him, that we may be also glorified together" (Romans 8:17).

Reflection: *"Buried under the biggest burden is a good place to find an even greater blessing"* (Janette Oke).

18

JOY—THE JOY OF THE LORD IS YOUR STRENGTH

But let all who put their trust in thee rejoice: let them ever shout for joy, because thou defendest them: let them also that love thy name be joyful in thee. for thou, Lord, wilt bless the righteous; with favour wilt thou compass him as with a shield.

(Psalm 5:11-12)

Central Truth: God's joy deep within you is a source of great strength and happiness. Be joyful in Him.

Central Focus: I am truly joyful because God has blessed me and surrounded me with His favor. I will walk in joy today and always.

Prayer: Father, thank you for imparting your joy to me. I will ever rejoice because of your blessings in my life and because I know you. I will shout for joy, because I know you defend me. I love your name and I am joyful in you. Thank you for surrounding me with your favor as with a shield.

You will show me the path of life. In your presence there is fullness of joy and at your right hand there are pleasures forevermore. Hallelujah! Though weeping may endure through the night, I know that your joy will come in the morning. Your mercy encompasses me, and this knowledge makes me want to shout for joy.

I am so glad, Father, and I want to always follow your righteous cause. I will magnify you, and my tongue will speak of your righteousness and praise all day long. O send out your light and truth. Let them lead me. Let them bring me unto your holy hill and to your tabernacles. Then I will go to your altar, Father, for you are my exceeding joy.

I will ever praise you, O Lord my God. I hope in you and will praise you, for you are the health of my countenance and my God. Hallelujah! Restore unto me the joy of your salvation and uphold me with your free Spirit. My soul will ever be joyful in you, O Lord.

My soul shall be satisfied and my mouth shall praise you with joyful lips. Father, I will make a joyful noise unto you and sing forth the honor of your name. I will make a joyful noise to you, the rock of my salvation. I will come before your presence with thanksgiving and make a joyful noise to you with Psalms, for you are a great God and a great King above all gods. Hallelujah!

Thank you for taking pleasure in your people, Lord, and beautifying the meek with your salvation. I will be joyful in glory and I will sing aloud upon my bed. I will let your high praises be in my mouth, and I will carry a two-edged sword in my hand.

Thank you for making me a joyful person, Father.

In the joyful name of Jesus I pray, Amen.

Scriptures: Psalm 5; Psalm 16; Psalm 30; Psalm 32; Psalm 35; Psalm 43; Psalm 51; Psalm 53; Psalm 63;

Psalm 66; Psalm 95; Psalm 149.

Personal Affirmation: From this day forward I will walk in the joy of the Lord, which truly is my strength. (See Nehemiah 8:10.) Knowing the Lord is joy unspeakable that is full of glory. (See 1 Peter 1:8.)

New Testament Scripture: "Whom having not seen, ye love; in whom, though now ye see him not, yet believing, ye rejoice with joy unspeakable and full of glory" (1 Peter 1:8).

Reflection: *"Joy is the serious business of Heaven"* (C. S. Lewis).

19
KEEPING POWER—GOD IS HOLDING ON TO YOU AND KEEPING YOU

Keep me as the apple of the eye, hide me under the shadow of thy wings.
(Psalm 17:8)

Central Truth: God keeps you in the hollow of His hand. Reach out and take hold of His hand. He will keep you, help you, and be with you throughout your life. His keeping power cannot fail.

Central Focus: The Lord is my Keeper. He will sustain me and see me through all of like's difficulties. As I commit my way to Him, I know He will keep me in His hand, as the apple of His eye.

Prayer: O Lord my God, I thank you for your keeping power in my life. Thank you for preserving me. It thrills me to know that you are keeping me as the apple of your eye, and you are hiding me under the shadow of your wings.

Keep me from presumptuous sins. Let them not have dominion over me. Let the words of my mouth and the meditation of my heart be acceptable in your sight, O Lord, my strength and my Redeemer. O keep my soul and deliver me. Let me not be ashamed, for I put my trust in you. Let integrity and uprightness preserve me, for I wait on you.

Keep me, O Lord, from the hands of the wicked, and preserve me from violent people. Let my prayer be set forth before you as incense, and the lifting up of my hands as the evening sacrifice. Set a watch, O Lord, before my mouth. Keep the door of my lips.

It makes me happy to keep your ways, Lord, and to seek you with all my heart. This is your keeping power at work in my life. Help me to obey you and to keep your commandments at all times. I will keep your statutes. Do not forsake me.

Take not the word of truth out of my mouth, for I have hoped in your judgments. Thank you, Father. It is my desire to keep your Word forever.

Thank you for your keeping power in my life.

In Jesus' name, Amen.

Scriptures: Psalm 12; Psalm 17; Psalm 19; Psalm 25; Psalm 140; Psalm 141; Psalm 119.

Personal Affirmation: God is keeping me, and He will keep me forever. I yield myself to Him. I know He will preserve me, watch over me, and keep me. He is so faithful to me.

New Testament Scripture: "And the peace of God, which passeth all understanding, shall keep your hearts and minds through Jesus Christ" (Philippians 4:7).

Reflection: *"Almighty God is on our team. He is our faithful Sustainer. When everybody else abandons us, we can count on Him. When nobody else is willing*

*to endure with us, He is there. He is trustworthy,
reliable, and consistent. We can depend on Him"*
(Charles Stanley).

20
LEADING OF THE LORD— FOLLOWING HIM EACH STEP OF THE WAY

Lead me, O Lord, in thy righteousness
because of mine enemies;
Make thy way straight before my face.
(Psalm 5:8)

Central Truth: God is surely leading you. Be sure to follow Him each step of the way.

Central Focus: God is leading me, and this truly is a blessed realization in my life. He leads me in the path of righteousness for His name's sake.

Prayer: Lead me, O Lord, in your righteousness. Show me your ways, and teach me your paths. Lead me in your truth and teach me, for you are the God of my salvation, and I wait on you all day long. Teach me your way, O Lord, and lead me in a plain path. I will wait upon you and be of good courage, for I know you are strengthening my heart.

I place all my trust in you, O Lord. Never let me be ashamed. Deliver me in your righteousness. Bow down your ear to me. Deliver me speedily. Be my strong Rock and my fortress. For your name's sake lead me and guide me.

O send out your light and your truth. Let them lead

me. Let them bring me unto your holy hill and to your tabernacles. Then I will go unto your altar, O God, for you are my exceeding joy. I will praise you, O God my God.

Hear my cry, O God. Attend unto my prayer. Lead me to the Rock that is higher than I. Thank you for being my shelter and a strong tower from the enemy. Search me, O God, and know my heart. Try me and know my thoughts, and see if there is any wicked way in me. Lead me in your everlasting way.

Teach me to do your will, for you are my God. Your Spirit is good. Lead me into the land of uprightness. How I thank you that you lead me by the still waters, and you lead me in the paths of righteousness for your name's sake. Hallelujah!

Where you lead me I will follow, Father. Continue your excellent leadership in my life.

In the precious name of Jesus I pray, Amen.

Scriptures: Psalm 5; Psalm 25; Psalm 27; Psalm 31; Psalm 43; Psalm 61; Psalm 139; Psalm 143; Psalm 23.

Personal Affirmation: I will follow the Lord each step of the way, and I will continually seek His leadership in my life. He will ever be my leader. I will walk in His righteousness, blessing, and love.

New Testament Scripture: "The sheep hear his voice: and he calleth his own sheep by name, and leadeth them out. And when he putteth forth his own sheep, he goeth before them, and the sheep follow him: for they know his voice" (John 10:3-5).

Reflection: *"The man that believes will obey. God gives faith to the obedient heart only. Where real repentance is, there is obedience"* (A.W. Tozer).

21
LOVE—
THE MARK OF A TRUE DISCIPLE

I will love thee, O Lord, my strength.
The Lord is my rock, and my fortress, and my
deliverer; my God, my strength, in whom I will
trust; my buckler, and the horn of my salvation,
and my high tower.
(Psalm 18:1-2)

Central Truth: Love comes from God. It is through love that we show that we are the children of God. Love, love, love!

Central Focus: God is love, and in His love I find my reason for being. I will walk in His love each step of my way, and I will share His love with others. I want to know more and more about His wonderful love.

Prayer: I will love you, O Lord, my strength. You are my rock, my fortress, and my deliverer. You are my God and my strength, and I will ever trust in you. You are my buckler, the horn of my salvation, and my high tower. I love you, O Lord.

Let all those who put their trust in you rejoice, dear Father, and let them ever shout for joy. Thank you for defending me. I love your name, and I will be joyful in you. Hallelujah! As I seek you, Father, I rejoice and am glad in you. I love your salvation, and I want you to be magnified in my life.

I set my love upon you, Father, and as I do so, I know you will deliver me. Thank you for your promise to set me on high because I have known your name. As I call upon you, I know you will answer me. You will be with me in times of trouble and you will deliver me. Thank you for your promise to satisfy me with long life.

I love you, Lord, because you have heard my voice and my supplications. Praise your mighty name! Because you have inclined your ear unto me, I will call upon you as long as I live. I believe your promise, Father, your promise that says that all those who love you will prosper. Thank you, Lord.

Thank you for your promise to preserve me. My mouth shall speak of your praise and bless your holy name forever.

In your loving name I pray, Amen.

Scriptures: Psalm 18; Psalm 5; Psalm 69; Psalm 70; Psalm 91; Psalm 116; Psalm 122; Psalm 145.

Personal Affirmation: I know God loves me with an everlasting love. I will walk in His love each step of my way. His love lifts me up and keeps me keeping on. I will ever be thankful for God's love in my life.

New Testament Scripture: "By this shall all men know that ye are my disciples, if ye have love one to another" (John 13:35).

Reflection: *"We ought to love our Maker for His*

own sake, without either hope of good or fear of pain" (Cervantes).

22
LOVING-KINDNESS— HIS LOVING-KINDNESS IS BETTER THAN LIFE

How excellent is thy lovingkindness, O God!
Therefore the children of men put their trust under
the shadow of your wings.
(Psalm 36:7)

Central Truth: God loves you! You can depend upon His kindness. His loving-kindness is better than life!

Central Focus: God's loving-kindness is always there for me. It is such a special treasure in my life. I will walk in His loving-kindness and share it with others.

Prayer: Show forth your loving-kindness, O God. Keep me as the apple of your eye, and hide me under the shadow of your wings. Your loving-kindness is before my eyes, as I walk in your truth. How excellent is your loving-kindness, O God. I put my trust under the shadow of your wings. Thank you, Father.

I have not hid your righteousness within my heart. I have declared your faithfulness and your salvation. I will never conceal your loving-kindness and your truth. Thank you, Father. Do not withhold your tender mercies from me, O God, and let your loving-kindness and your truth continually preserve me.

Have mercy upon me, O God, according to your

loving-kindnesses. According to the multitude of your tender mercies, blot out all my transgressions. Wash me thoroughly from my iniquity and cleanse me from my sin, for I acknowledge my transgressions, and my sin is ever before me.

Because your loving-kindness is better than life, my lips shall praise you. Thus will I bless you while I live; I will lift up my hands in your name. Hallelujah! Hear me, O Lord, for your loving-kindness is good. Turn unto me according to the multitude of your tender mercies.

It is a good thing to give thanks to you, O Lord, and to sing praises to your name, O Most High. I will show forth your loving-kindness in the morning and your faithfulness every night. Thank you for crowning me with your loving-kindness and tender mercies. I love you, Father-God.

Teach me to do your will, for you are my God. Your Spirit is good. Lead me into the land of uprightness. Quicken me, O Lord, for your name's sake. For your righteousness' sake, bring my soul out of trouble. Cause me to hear your loving-kindness in the morning, for I trust completely in you. Cause me to know the way in which I should walk, for I lift up my soul to you.

Thank you for your loving-kindness in my life, dear God.

In the name of the loving Savior I pray, Amen.

Scriptures: Psalm 17; Psalm 26; Psalm 36; Psalm 40; Psalm 51; Psalm 56; Psalm 63; Psalm 69; Psalm 103; Psalm 148.

Personal Affirmation: I benefit from God's loving-kindness every day of my life. I will let His loving-kindness flow forth from me to others.

New Testament Scripture: "Herein is love, not that we loved God, but that he loved us, and sent his Son to be the propitiation for our sins" (1 John 4:10).

Reflection: *"Pour through me now; I yield myself to Thee, O Love that led my Lord to Calvary"* (Amy Carmichael).

23

Magnifying the Lord— Making Him Bigger and Greater

O magnify the Lord with me, and let us exalt his name together.
(Psalm 34:3)

Central Truth: We magnify and exalt the Lord through praise, worship, and witnessing. He is great and greatly to be praised, and the more we praise Him, the bigger He becomes to us.

Central Focus: I will magnify the Lord through prayer, praise, and worship. As I do so, He is becoming greater and greater to me.

Prayer: Lord God, you are great and greatly to be praised. I choose to magnify you and to exalt your name. As I do so, you are becoming bigger and greater to me. Thank you, Father.

I will shout for joy and be glad in you, as I favor your righteous cause, O Lord. I choose to magnify you continually, because I know you take pleasure in me. This is so wonderful to know. It is my heart's desire, dear Father, to speak of your righteousness and your praise all day long. Hallelujah!

As I seek you, I rejoice in you. I love the salvation you've given to me. Help me to remember to say continually,

"The Lord be magnified!" Thank you for thinking about me. You are my help and my deliverer. I know you will not tarry, O God.

May you ever be magnified through my praise and life, dear Father. I will praise you with my whole heart. I will worship toward your holy temple, and I will praise your name for your loving-kindness and for your truth. I thank you that you have magnified your Word above your name. In your Word I find the strength I need.

I will praise you with a song and I will magnify you with thanksgiving. I want to magnify you at all times, dear Lord. It is my desire to please you. In you I place all my trust. Let me never be put to confusion. Deliver me in your righteousness. Incline your ear to me and save me.

I thank you that you are my strong habitation, and I will continually resort to you. You are my rock and my fortress. You are my hope, O God, and you are my trust from my youth. Let my mouth be filled with your praise and with your honor all day long.

My mouth will show forth your righteousness and your salvation, as I go forth in your strength. Your righteousness, O God, is very high, and you have done so many great things. Praise your name! There is no one who is like you, O God.

I bless you and magnify you. I give you the honor that is due your name. I praise you and walk with you every step of my way.

In the magnificent name of Jesus I pray, Amen.

Scriptures: Psalm 48; Psalm 34; Psalm 35; Psalm 40; Psalm 70; Psalm 138; Psalm 69; Psalm 71.

Personal Affirmation: I will magnify the Lord and exalt His precious name throughout this day!

New Testament Scripture: "According to my earnest expectation and my hope, that in nothing I shall be ashamed, but that with all boldness, as always, so now also Christ shall be magnified in my body, whether it be by life, or by death" (Philippians 1:20).

Reflection: *"Then you will behold God, good not through the having of any other good thing, but He is the goodness of every good"* (St. Augustine).

24

MAJESTY OF GOD—GLORIFYING HIM THROUGH PRAYER

The Lord reigneth, he is clothed with majesty; the Lord is clothed with strength, wherewith he hath girded himself; the world also is established, that it cannot be moved. Thy throne is established of old: thou art from everlasting.
(Psalm 93:1-2)

Central Truth: God is the majestic, sovereign Ruler of the universe. Bow your heart before Him as you pray.

Central Focus: God in all His majesty should be the focus of my attention all day long. He is my King, and His kingdom will endure forever. I choose to worship Him in all his majesty, glory, and radiance.

Prayer: Father-God, you are the majestic Creator of the universe, and you are my God and King. I worship you in spirit and truth. You are clothed with majesty and strength, O God. I adore you as I bow before you. I thank you that you reign over me and all the world.

I will give you the glory that is due to your name, O Father, and I will worship you in the beauty of holiness. Your voice is upon the waters, and it is powerful and full of majesty. Glory to your holy name. Thank you for the strength and peace you have imparted to me.

Your throne, O God, is forever and ever. As you reign, you are clothed with majesty, O Lord, and you are clothed with strength. You are mightier than many waters and the waves of the sea. I honor your majesty, O God.

I sing a new song unto you, O God, and I bless your name. I will declare your glory and your wonders among all people. You are so great, and you are greatly to be praised. I respect you and honor you. Honor and majesty are before you, O Lord. Strength and beauty are in your sanctuary.

Glory and strength are yours, Father, as I worship you in the beauty of holiness. You reign forever. Blessed be your name. I rejoice in you. I bless you from the depths of my soul, for you are very great, and you are clothed with honor and majesty. You cover yourself with light as though it is your garment. Praise your holy name.

I will extol you, O God, my King. I will bless your name forever and ever. I will bless you every day, and I will praise your name forever and ever. I thank you for your greatness, which truly is unsearchable. I will speak of the glorious honor of your majesty and of all your wondrous works.

I thank you for being so gracious and full of compassion. You are slow to anger and of great mercy. You are good to all, Father, and your tender mercies are over all your works. Thank you for always being near to me, as I call upon you in truth.

Help me to make known to others how mighty you are and to let them know about the majesty of your kingdom, which is an everlasting kingdom, and your dominion endures throughout all generations.

I bow before you, my majestic Father.

In Jesus' name I pray, Amen.

Scriptures: Psalm 92; Psalm 29; Psalm 45; Psalm 93; Psalm 96; Psalm 97; Psalm 104; Psalm 145.

Personal Affirmation: I will worship at the footstool of the majestic sovereign of the universe—the King of kings and the Lord of lords.

New Testament Scripture: "For we have not followed cunningly devised fables, when we made known unto you the power and coming of our Lord Jesus Christ, but were eyewitnesses of his majesty. For he received from God the Father honour and glory, when there came such a voice to him from the excellent glory, This is my beloved Son, in whom I am well pleased" (2 Peter 1:16-17).

Reflection: *"To say that God is sovereign is to declare that . . . whatever takes place in time is but the outworking of that which He decreed in eternity"* (A. W. Pink).

25

MEDITATION—REFLECTING UPON THE GOODNESS OF GOD

But his delight is in the law of the Lord; and in his law doth he meditate day and night.
(Psalm 1:2)

Central Truth: As we meditate upon God and His Word, we grow strong and mature. Meditation gives us renewed minds and supernatural peace.

Central Focus: Meditation is the doorway to spiritual understanding. I want to learn to meditate upon the Word of God both night and day. Praying His Word enables me to meditate more fully and effectively.

Prayer: O God, my heavenly Father, thank you for always being there for me. I bow before you. Help me never to walk in the counsel of the ungodly, to stand in the way of sinners, or to sit in the seat of the scornful. I find my delight in your Word, and I will meditate in your Word day and night.

You are my God, and I will seek you early each day. My soul thirsts for you, and my flesh longs for you. It is my desire to see your power and glory. Your loving-kindness is better than life to me, and my lips shall praise you. I will bless you while I live, and I will lift up my hands in your name. My mouth shall praise you with joyful lips as I meditate upon you during the night.

I will ever remember your works, O Most High, and I will meditate upon your wonders. Indeed, I will meditate upon all your work and all your doings. You are my great God, and I adore you. You are the God who does wonders, and you have blessed your people with strength. Thank you, Father.

Thank you for your Word, which is a lamp unto my feet and a light unto my path. I will meditate upon your precepts, Father. I will meditate upon your Word each day. The heavens declare your glory, and the firmament shows forth your handiwork. Let the words of my mouth and the meditation of my heart be acceptable in your sight, O Lord, my strength and my redeemer.

My mouth shall speak of your wisdom, and the meditation of my heart shall be of understanding. Thank you, Father. I will sing unto you, Lord, as long as I live. I will sing praise to you while I have my being. My meditation of you shall be sweet, and I will be glad in you.

Bless the Lord, O my soul. Praise your mighty name!

In the name of Jesus I pray, Amen.

Scriptures: Psalm 1; Psalm 63; Psalm 77; Psalm 119; Psalm 19; Psalm 49; Psalm 104.

Personal Affirmation: I will meditate upon God and His Word throughout the day. I will renew my mind by washing it in the water of God's Word.

New Testament Scripture: "Meditate upon these things;

give thyself wholly to them; that thy profiting may appear to all" (1 Timothy 4:15).

Reflection: *"You should arrange yourself and all your thoughts and actions as if today you were going to die"* (Thomas a Kempis).

26
MERCY—GOD'S MERCY IS FREELY AVAILABLE TO YOU

Hear me when I call, O God of my righteousness:
thou hast enlarged me when I was in distress; have
mercy upon me, and hear my prayer.
(Psalm 4:1)

Central Truth: God's mercy is from everlasting to everlasting. To walk in His mercy we must be merciful.

Central Focus: Mercy is always triumphant over judgment. Mercy involves kindness, compassion, and love. With God's help I will become a merciful person.

Prayer: O Lord, my merciful God, help me to walk in mercy. Have mercy upon me, for I am weak. I trust in your mercy, and my heart rejoices in your salvation. I will sing unto you, O Lord, for you have always dealt bountifully with me. Thank you, Father.

Surely goodness and mercy shall follow me all the days of my life, and I will dwell in your house forever. Praise your holy name! Show me your ways, O Lord, and teach me your paths. Lead me in your truth and teach me, for you are the God of my salvation, and I wait on you all day long. Remember, O Lord, your tender mercies and your loving-kindnesses, for they have been ever of old.

Father, I will be glad and rejoice in your mercy, for I know you have considered my troubles, and you have known my soul in the midst of adversities. I know that your eye is upon me, O Lord, as I hope in your mercy.

You are my defense, O God, and I will wait upon you. You are the God of mercy, and I will ever sing unto you. Thank you for being my defense and the God of my mercy. Revive me, that I would rejoice in you, O Lord, and show me your mercy. It blesses me to know that mercy and truth have met together and righteousness and peace have kissed each other in you. Hallelujah!

Teach me your way, O God, I will walk in your truth. Unite my heart to fear your name. I will praise you, O Lord my God, with all my heart, and I will glorify your name forevermore. How I thank you for the great mercy you've given to me. You are full of compassion, O God, and you are gracious, long-suffering, and plenteous in mercy and truth. Thank you so much for being who you are to me.

I come into your presence with singing, mighty Father. I know you are the God who has made me. I am a sheep in your pasture. I enter your gates with thanksgiving and go into your courts with praise. I am thankful unto you and I bless your holy name. You are so good to me, and your mercy is everlasting. I thank you that your truth endures to all generations.

Thank you for taking pleasure in me, Lord, as I learn to fear you and hope in your mercy. Deal with me according to your mercy, Father, and teach me your statutes. I am your servant; give me understanding, that I may know your Word. It is time for you to work,

O Lord, and I know you will take action in my behalf.

In the precious, most merciful name of Jesus I pray, Amen.

Scriptures: Psalm 6; Psalm 13; Psalm 23; Psalm 25; Psalm 31; Psalm 33; Psalm 59; Psalm 85; Psalm 86; Psalm 100; Psalm 147; Psalm 119.

Personal Affirmation: I will sing of the mercies of the Lord forever. I will walk in His mercy and extend His mercy to others. Surely goodness and mercy will follow me all the days of my life, and I will dwell in the house of the Lord forever.

New Testament Scripture: "Blessed be the God and Father of our Lord Jesus Christ, which according to His abundant mercy hath begotten us again unto a lively hope by the resurrection of Jesus Christ from the dead" (1 Peter 1:3).

Reflection: *"The Lord's goodness surrounds us at every moment. I walk through it almost with difficulty, as through thick grass and flowers"* (R. W. Barbour).

27
PEACE—LEARNING TO REST IN THE LORD

The Lord will give strength unto his people; the Lord will bless his people with peace.
(Psalm 29:11)

Central Truth: To know God is to experience His peace every moment of the day. Without Him, there can be no peace.

Central Focus: Peace is a fruit of the Holy Spirit in my life. His supernatural peace floods my being, and I will walk in the peace He has imparted to me. As I pray, I find His peace.

Prayer: God of all peace, I give my life and heart to you afresh. I love you, and I thank you for the peace you have imparted unto me. Thank you for giving me your peace and strength.

You have put gladness in my heart, and I will lie down in peace and sleep, because I know you cause me to dwell in safety. Thank you, Father. Help me to keep my tongue from evil and my lips from speaking guile. I will depart from evil and do good. Through your grace, Father, I will seek and pursue peace.

Thank you for your promise that the meek will inherit the Earth and shall delight themselves in the abundance of peace. Hallelujah! Thank you for the great peace you have given to me, because I love your Word. Your Word gives me peace.

Thank you, Lord, for allowing me to flourish in your righteousness and blessing me with abundant peace. I will sing of your mercies forever, Father, and with my mouth I will make known your faithfulness to all generations. Hold not your peace, O God of my praise.

I love your Word, and this gives me great peace. Thank you for your Word, dear Father. I was glad when they said unto me, "Let us go into the house of the Lord." I pray for the peace of Jerusalem and for her prosperity as well.

I will praise you with my whole heart. I will worship toward your holy temple and praise your name for your loving-kindness, peace, and truth. Thank you for magnifying your Word above all your name. Thank you for answering my prayers and strengthening me with great strength in my soul.

O Lord, you have searched me and known me. You know when I sit down and when I rise up. You understand my thoughts from afar. Praise your holy name.

How precious are your thoughts to me, O God, and how great is the sum of them. Search me, O God, and know my heart: try me, and know my thoughts. See if there be any wicked way in me and lead me in the everlasting path.

In the peaceful name of Jesus, the Prince of

Peace, I pray, Amen.

Scriptures: Psalm 29; Psalm 4; Psalm 34; Psalm 37; Psalm 119; Psalm 72; Psalm 109; Psalm 119; Psalm 122; Psalm 138; Psalm 139.

Personal Affirmation: Because I know God will keep me in perfect peace as I learn to trust in Him, I will trust Him and walk in peace from this time forward.

New Testament Scripture: "Peace I leave with you, my peace I give unto you: not as the world giveth, give I unto you. Let not your heart be troubled, neither let it be afraid" (John 14:27).

Reflection: *"All men who live with any degree of serenity live by some assurance of grace. In every life there must at least be times and seasons when the good is felt as a present possession and not as a far-off goal"* (Reinhold Niebuhr).

28
PRAISE—
GIVING GOD HIS DUE

Make a joyful noise unto God, all ye lands;
Sing forth the honour of his name:
make his praise glorious.
(Psalm 66:1-2)

Central Truth: Praising God involves thanking Him for all He's done and worshiping Him for who He is.

Central Focus: Praising God is one of the best things you can do throughout the day. It produces better health, happiness, and peace. Praising God draws you into His presence.

Prayer: O God of might and glory, I will praise you according to your righteousness. I will sing praise to you, O Most High. I will praise you with my whole heart and show forth all your marvelous works. I will be glad and rejoice in you. I will sing praise to your name, O Most High.

You are my strength and my shield, O Lord. My heart trusts in you. Therefore, my heart greatly rejoices, and with my song I will praise you. I will bless you at all times, and your praise shall continually be in my mouth. My soul shall make its boast in you. The humble will hear thereof and be glad.

I will praise you forever, dear Lord, because of all the

things you've done. I will wait on you. O God, you are my God. Early will I seek you. Because your loving-kindness is better than life to me, my lips shall praise you, and thus will I bless you while I live. I will lift up my hands in your name.

Praise waits for you, O God. I will praise you with my whole heart in the assembly of the upright. I will praise you, for I am fearfully and wonderfully made by your hands, dear Father. Marvelous are your works!

I will extol you, my God, and I will bless your name forever. Every day I will bless you, and I will praise you forever and ever. You are great and greatly to be praised. As I praise you, I sing unto you a new song.

How I thank you that you take pleasure in your people and beautify the meek with your salvation. I will be joyful in the glory you've imparted to me. I will sing aloud upon my bed. I will let your high praises be in my mouth and a two-edged sword will be in my hands.

I praise you, Lord, in the sanctuary. I praise you in the firmament of your power. I praise you for your mighty acts. I praise you according to your excellent greatness. Praise ye the Lord!

In Jesus' name I pray, Amen.

Scriptures: Psalm 7; Psalm 9; Psalm 28; Psalm 34; Psalm 52; Psalm 63; Psalm 65; Psalm 111; Psalm 139; Psalm 145; Psalm 150.

Personal Affirmation: I will praise the Lord at all times.

His praise shall continually be in my mouth.

New Testament Scripture: "And a voice came out of the throne, saying, Praise our God, all ye his servants, and ye that fear him, both small and great" (Revelation 19:5).

Reflection: *"In the interior life of prayer [and praise] faithfulness points steadily to God and His purposes, away from self and its preoccupations"* (Evelyn Underhill).

29
Prayer—
Dialogue With God

Hear me when I call, O God of my righteousness:
thou hast enlarged me when I was in distress; have
mercy upon me, and hear my prayer.
(Psalm 4:1)

Central Truth: Prayer gives you a direct line to your Father in Heaven.

Central Focus: Prayer is vitally important to the spirit of man in the same sense that air is vital to a person's body. It is the Christian's "native air."

Prayer: Give ear to my words, O Lord, consider my meditation. Hearken unto the voice of my cry, my King and my God, for unto you I will pray. You will hear my voice in the morning, O Lord. In the morning I will direct my prayer unto you, and I will look up. Praise your holy name.

Lord, I know you have heard my supplications and you will receive my prayer. Thank you for always being there for me. As I cast my burdens upon you, I know you will sustain me. Let my prayer come before you. Incline your ear unto my cry.

I give myself unto prayer, dear Father. You are my God; hear the voice of my supplication. I cry unto you. Make haste unto me. Give ear unto my voice when I cry unto you. Let my prayer be set forth before you as incense and the lifting up of my hands as the evening sacrifice.

Set a watch, O Lord, before my mouth. Keep the door of my lips. As I cry unto you, I realize afresh that you are my refuge and my portion in the land of the living. Attend unto my cry. In your faithfulness and righteousness I ask you to answer me.

As for me, I will call upon you, O God, and I know you will hear me and intervene in my life. Evening and morning and at noon I will pray and cry aloud to you, and I know you will hear my voice. Hear my voice, O God, in my prayer. Preserve my life from fear of the enemy.

Give ear, O shepherd of Israel, you who dwell between the cherubim. Turn me again, O God, and cause your face to shine. O Lord God of hosts, thank you for taking me from strength to strength. Hear my prayer and give ear to me.

O God my shield. Look upon my face. I realize that a day in your courts is better than a thousand elsewhere. I had rather be a doorkeeper in your house, O Lord, than to dwell in the tents of wickedness. You are my sun and my shield, and you will impart your grace and glory to me.

It is so wonderful to know that you will not withhold any good thing from me as I walk uprightly before you. O Lord of hosts, trusting in you blesses me through and through.

In the blessed name of Jesus, who taught me to pray, Amen.

Scriptures: Psalm 5; Psalm 6; Psalm 55; Psalm 88; Psalm 109; Psalm 141; Psalm 142; Psalm 143; Psalm 64; Psalm 80.

Personal Affirmation: I will adore the Lord. I will pray without ceasing. I will confess my sins to Him. I will express thanksgiving to Him. I will praise His holy name. I will ask Him to supply my needs, and I know He will respond to my prayers. Hallelujah!

New Testament Scripture: "Continue in prayer, and watch in the same with thanksgiving" (Colossians 4:2).

Reflection: *"Prayer is not a discourse. It is a form of life, the life with God. That is why it is not confined to the moment of verbal statement"* (Jacques Ellul).

30
PRESENCE OF GOD—
THE BEST PLACE TO BE

Thou wilt shew me the path of life: in thy presence is fullness of joy; At thy right hand there are pleasures for evermore.
(Psalm 16:11)

Central Truth: Abiding in God's presence gives you peace, direction, security, and spiritual understanding.

Central Focus: I love being in God's presence where I find fullness of joy and pleasures forevermore. I want to abide in His presence forevermore.

Prayer: Thank you, Father, for enabling me to go into your presence. In your wonderful presence I find fullness of joy and pleasures forevermore. It is so delightful to be in your presence.

In you I place all my trust, Lord God. Let me never be ashamed. Be my strong rock; you are my fortress. Lead me and guide me. Into your hand I commit my spirit. Thank you for redeeming me, O Lord God of truth.

Oh, how great is your goodness, which you have laid up for them that fear you. You shall hide me in your presence. Blessed are you, O Lord, for you have shown me your marvelous kindness. Thank you, Father. I love you, Lord God. Thank you for preserving me and plentifully rewarding me.

Through your grace I will be of good courage. Strengthen my heart, O Lord, as I continue to hope in you. Create in me a clean heart, O God, and renew a right spirit within me. Do not cast me away from your presence.

I come to you with singing in my heart, and I make a joyful noise unto you, for you are the Rock of my salvation. I come before your presence with thanksgiving and I make a joyful noise to you with Psalms. You are a great God and a great King above all gods.

I serve you with gladness, Father, and I come before your presence with thanksgiving. You are my Creator, and I am a sheep in your pasture. I enter your gates with thanksgiving and I go into your courts with praise. I am so thankful unto you, and I bless your holy name. You are so good, Lord, and your mercy is everlasting. I thank you that your truth endures to all generations.

I will ever give thanks unto your name, as I dwell continually in your presence. Hallelujah!

In the name of Jesus I pray, Amen.

Scriptures: Psalm 16; Psalm 31; Psalm 51; Psalm 95; Psalm 100; Psalm 140.

Personal Affirmation: I will practice the presence of God throughout my life.

New Testament Scripture: "Now unto him that is able to keep you from falling, and to present you faultless before the presence of his glory with exceeding joy, to the only wise God our Saviour, be glory and majesty, dominion and power, both now and ever. Amen" (Jude 24).

Reflection: *"The presence of God is the life and nourishment of the soul"* (Brother Lawrence).

31

QUICKENING— GOD'S LIFE-GIVING POWER

Quicken me after thy lovingkindness;
so shall I keep the testimony of thy mouth.
(Psalm 119:88)

Central Truth: God's power is at work within you and this gives life to your soul and body.

Central Focus: It is in God that we live and move and have our being. His power strengthens us and quickens our mortal bodies.

Prayer: O Lord, my God, I ask you to quicken me after your loving-kindness. I know you will quicken me, increase my greatness, and comfort me on every side. I will ever praise you, O Holy One of Israel. My lips shall greatly rejoice when I sing unto you.

Father, I will never turn away from you. Quicken me and I will call upon your name. Turn me, Lord, and cause your face to shine. Quicken me according to your Word. Make me understand the way of your precepts, so shall I talk of your wondrous works.

Turn my eyes away from beholding vanity, Father, and quicken me in the way. Establish your Word within me, for I am your servant. I have longed after your precepts; quicken me in your righteousness. Quicken me, O Lord, according to your Word.

Hear my voice according unto your loving-kindness. O Lord, quicken me according to your judgment. Plead my cause and deliver me. Quicken me according to your Word. Great are your tender mercies, my God. Quicken me according to your judgments. Consider how I love your precepts, and quicken me, O Lord, according to your loving-kindness. Your Word is true from the beginning and every one of your righteous judgments endures forever.

Thank you for quickening me, dear Father. I love you so much.

In Jesus' name I pray, Amen.

Scriptures: Psalm 119; Psalm 71.

Personal Affirmation: Each day I will be filled afresh with the Holy Spirit, who is the quickening power of the Lord within me.

New Testament Scripture: "But if the Spirit of him that raised up Jesus from the dead dwell in you, he that raised up Christ from the dead shall also quicken your mortal bodies by his Spirit that dwelleth in you" (Romans 8:11).

Reflection: *"The life Christ lived qualified Him for the death He died—and the death He died qualifies us for the life we live" (Anonymous).*

32
REDEMPTION—
WE HAVE BEEN BOUGHT BACK
BY THE REDEEMER

Let the words of my mouth, and the meditation of my heart, be acceptable in thy sight, O Lord, my strength, and my redeemer.
(Psalm 19:14)

Central Truth: You have been redeemed by the grace of God.

Central Focus: God is my redeemer. Because of this I want to live a life that is pleasing to Him. I praise Him all day long.

Prayer: O Lord, my strength and my Redeemer, I do want the words of my mouth, the meditations of my heart, and the actions of my life to ever be acceptable to you. Praise your mighty name.

You are my rock, my high God, and my Redeemer. Thank you for buying me back from the hands of the enemy and for setting me free. Into your hands I commit my spirit, for I know you have redeemed me, O Lord God of truth.

I will be glad and rejoice in your mercy, for you have considered my troubles and you have known my soul. Thank you for your promise to increase my greatness and to comfort me on every side. I receive your promise as I pray. I will ever praise you, and sing unto you, O Holy One of Israel. My lips shall greatly rejoice when I sing unto you. My tongue shall talk of your righteousness all day long.

Thank you for your strong arm which has redeemed me from all evil. You are the God who does wonders, and you have declared your strength among the people. Thank you, Father.

Thank you for redeeming me from the hand of the enemy. I believe your words and I sing your praises. I give thanks to you, Lord God, for you are good, and your mercy endures forever. I have been redeemed by you and I will say so. I want others to know that you have redeemed me from the hand of the enemy. Thank you, Father.

Truly, I know your mercy endures forever. Thank you for remembering me when I was in a low estate and for redeeming me from all my enemies. I will give thanks to you, O God of Heaven, for your mercy endures forever. Hallelujah!

You have redeemed me and I will ever trust you. Because of this I know I will never be desolate. Thank you, Father. Thank you for forgiving me of all my iniquities and healing all my diseases. Thank you for redeeming my life from destruction and crowning me with your loving-kindness and tender mercies. Thank you for satisfying my mouth with good things, so that my youth is renewed like the eagle's.

Bless the Lord, O my soul, and all that is within me, bless His holy name. Bless the Lord, O my soul, and forget not all His benefits. I thank you so much that I have been redeemed.

In Jesus' name I pray, Amen.

Scriptures: Psalm 19; Psalm 78; Psalm 31; Psalm 71:21; Psalm 77; Psalm 106; Psalm 107; Psalm 136; Psalm 34; Psalm 103.

Personal Affirmation: Knowing that I have been redeemed makes me very happy and so thankful. I will ever rejoice in the knowledge of my redemption, and I will spend much time in the presence of my Redeemer.

New Testament Scripture: "In whom we have redemption through his blood, the forgiveness of sins, according to the riches of his grace" (Ephesians 1:7).

Reflection: *"The blood deals with what we have done, whereas the cross deals with what we are. The blood disposes of our sins, while the cross strikes at the root of our capacity for sin"* (Watchman Nee).

33
REFUGE—
THE LORD ALWAYS PROTECTS US

God is our refuge and strength,
a very present help in trouble.
(Psalm 46:1)

Central Truth: A refuge is shelter or protection from danger. God is my refuge, and because this is true, I shall not fear anything.

Central Focus: Taking refuge in the Lord is a matter of faith and trust. I choose to trust in Him and to take refuge in Him. As a result, peace is mine!

Prayer: Father, thank you for being my refuge and my strength. You are a very present help in times of trouble. Therefore, I shall not fear, no matter what happens. Through your grace I will be still and know that you are God.

I thank you for all the promises of your Word, which tell me that you are always willing to be a refuge for the oppressed, a refuge in times of trouble. This is wonderful to know, Father, and I take my refuge in you. I know your name, and I put my trust in you, for I know you will never forsake me.

Be merciful to me, O God, be merciful to me, for my soul trusts in you. In the shadow of your wings I will make my refuge. I will cry unto you, O Most High God, for you perform all things for me. I will sing of your power. I will sing aloud of your mercy, for you are my defense and my refuge. Unto you, O my strength, I will sing, for you are ever my defense and the God of my mercy. Hallelujah!

Truly my soul waits upon you, O Lord. My salvation comes from you. You only are my rock and my salvation. You are my defense; I shall not be moved. You are the rock of my strength and my refuge. I will trust in you at all times and pour out my heart before you.

Let my mouth be filled with your praise and honor every day, all day long. You are my strong refuge, and I praise you. I choose to dwell in your secret place, Almighty God, and to abide under your shadow. I will ever say that you are my refuge and my fortress and I will trust in you.

I know you will deliver me from the snare of the fowler and from the noisome pestilence. You will cover me with your feathers, and under your wings I will trust. You are my shield and buckler, and I shall not be afraid of the terror by night nor for the arrow that flies by day.

Thank you for your promises which tell me that no evil will befall me nor shall any plague come near my dwelling. I am so grateful to know that your angels will have charge over me, to keep me in all my ways. Praise the Lord!

Because I have set my love upon you, I know you will always deliver me. When I call upon you, I know you will answer me. Thank you for being with me in trouble, for delivering me, and for promising a long life to me.

You are my everlasting refuge, Lord, and I will ever abide in you.

In the name of Jesus I pray, Amen.

Scriptures: Psalm 46; Psalm 9; Psalm 57; Psalm 59; Psalm 62; Psalm 62; Psalm 71; Psalm 91.

Personal Affirmation: In God's presence I find peace, joy, and protection. I want to stay rooted and grounded in Him, for He is my refuge, my strength, and my fortress.

New Testament Scripture: "That by two immutable things in which it was impossible for God to lie, we might have a strong consolation, who have fled for refuge to lay hold upon the hope set before us; which hope we have as an anchor of the soul" (Hebrews 6:18-19).

Reflection: *"God loves each of us as if there were only one of us"* (Augustine).

34

REJOICING— THE MELODY OF THE HEART

But let those who put their trust in thee rejoice:
let them ever shout for joy, because thou
defendest them: let them also that love
thy name be joyful in thee.
(Psalm 5:11)

Central Truth: Rejoicing in the Lord is one of the best ways to spend our time and to use our lips, for as we rejoice in Him, our faith increases and our soul is restored.

Central Focus: We have so much to be thankful for. This leads us to rejoice in the Lord. Let us rejoice evermore!

Prayer: Father I put my trust in you. As I do so, my heart fills up with joy, and rejoicing is the overflow of that trust and joy within. Thank you for defending me. I love your name, and I shall ever be joyful in you. Thank you for your promise to bless me and to compass me about with your favor as with a shield. Hallelujah!

I will praise you, O Lord, with my whole heart. I will show forth all your marvelous works. I will be glad and rejoice in you. I will sing praise to your name, O Most High. I thank you for your mercy, Father, and I rejoice in your mercy, for you have considered my trouble. Thank you, Lord.

Your mercy truly does compass me about, Father, and I am glad in you. I shall ever rejoice and shout for joy because of all you've done for me. My heart rejoices in you, Father, because I have trusted in your holy name. Let your mercy be upon me, as I hope in you.

As I seek you, I rejoice in you. May you be magnified by my life and my words. This is the day that you have made, O Lord; I will rejoice and be glad in it. I rejoice at your Word, O Lord, as one who finds great spoil. Blessed are you, my Lord. Teach me your statutes. With my lips I have declared all the judgments of your mouth.

I have rejoiced in the way of your testimonies, as much as in all riches. I will meditate in your precepts, and I will have respect unto your ways. I will delight myself in your statutes, and I will not forget your Word.

I will bless you, O Lord. Thank you for giving me your counsel. I have set you before me, because you are at my right hand. Therefore, I shall not be moved. My heart is glad and my glory rejoices. My flesh shall also rest in hope. I know you will show me the path of life. In your presence there is fullness of joy, and at your right hand there are pleasures forevermore.

Scriptures: Psalm 5:11; Psalm 9; Psalm 31; Psalm 32; Psalm 33; Psalm 40; Psalm 119; Psalm 16.

Personal Affirmation: I have so many reasons to rejoice. I will rejoice evermore, for rejoicing helps me to see things more clearly and to know where the many blessings I enjoy come from.

New Testament Scripture: "Rejoice evermore. Pray without ceasing. In every thing give thanks: for this is the will of God in Christ Jesus concerning you" (1 Thessalonians 5:16-18).

Reflection: *"What makes a man's eighty-year-old Irish uncle skip like a little boy? 'Me Father is very fond of me!'"* (John Ortberg, Jr.).

35
REST—
GOD'S PROMISE TO YOU

Rest in the Lord, and wait patiently for him.
(Psalm 37:7)

Central Truth: God promises to give you rest, but you must lean on Him.

Central Focus: Learning to rest in God requires you to cease from your own striving.

Prayer: O God, I thank you for providing rest for my soul. I claim your promise of rest for every moment of every day. My heart is glad in you and my glory rejoices in you. My flesh rests in the hope you have given to me. Thank you for showing me the path of life. In your presence I experience fullness of joy and at your right hand I experience pleasures forevermore. Thank you, Father.

Father, I trust in you. It is my desire to always do good and to delight myself in you. As I do so, I know you will give me the desires of my heart. Praise your holy name! One of my heart's desires is to live in your rest, as I commit my way to you and trust in you.

You will surely bring it to pass in my life, Lord, and I know you will bring forth your righteousness in my life and your judgment as the noonday. Hallelujah! I take my rest in you, Lord, and I wait patiently for you. Thank you for your marvelous rest.

I come to you, and I sing unto you, my Father. I make a joyful noise to you, for you are the Rock of my salvation. I come before your presence with thanksgiving, and I make a joyful noise unto you with Psalms. You are a great God, a great King above all gods. Hallelujah!

In your hand are the deep places of the Earth. The strength of the hills is yours also. The sea is yours, and you made it. Your hands also formed the dry land. I worship and bow down in your presence, and this gives rest to me. I kneel before you, O Lord, my Maker.

I love you, Lord, because you have heard my voice and my supplications. Thank you for inclining your ear unto me.

Scriptures: Psalm 16; Psalm 37; Psalm 100; Psalm 95.

Personal Affirmation: I will rest in the Lord instead of striving in my own strength and desire.

New Testament Scripture: "Let us labour therefore to enter into that rest, lest any man fall after the same example of unbelief" (Hebrews 4:11).

Reflection: *"The Christian life is not by effort, and not by struggle; not merely by trying to put into practice certain maxims, or by trying to attain to a certain measure; but from beginning to end, and all together, it is a matter of knowing the Lord Jesus within"* (T. Austin Sparks).

36

RIGHTEOUSNESS—
WE ARE GOD'S RIGHTEOUSNESS
THROUGH CHRIST

Lead me, O Lord, in thy righteousness because of mine enemies; make thy way straight before my face.
(Psalm 5:8)

Central Truth: Jesus became sin for us, that we might become the righteousness of God in Him.

Central Focus: Righteousness is a state of being—the state of being we acquire when we permit Christ to become our Savior and Lord.

Prayer: O God of my righteousness, I come to you with deep gratitude in my heart for allowing me to become your righteousness through Christ. Hear me when I call, O God of my righteousness: you have enlarged me when I was in distress. Have mercy upon me, and hear my prayer.

I offer unto you, my God, the sacrifices of righteousness as I put my complete trust in you. Judge me, O Lord, according to my righteousness and according to my integrity within me. I will praise you according to your righteousness, and I will sing praise to your name, O Most High.

You, O righteous Lord, love righteousness, and I am thankful that your countenance beholds me. Help me to walk uprightly, to work righteousness, and to speak truth in my heart. As for me, I will behold your face in righteousness. I shall be satisfied when I awake with your likeness.

You are my Shepherd, O Lord, and I shall not want. You make me to lie down in green pastures, and lead me beside the still waters. You restore my soul and lead me in the paths of righteousness for your name's sake. Thank you, Father.

My tongue shall speak of your righteousness and of your praise all day long. I delight myself in you, O Lord. Thank you for your promise to give me the desires of my heart as I do so. I commit my way unto you, I trust in you, and I know you will bring answers to my prayers. Bring forth your righteousness as the light and your judgment as the noonday.

Be my strong foundation, Father, and I will continually come to you, for you are my rock and my fortress. My mouth shall show forth your righteousness and your salvation all the day long. I will go forth in your strength, O God, and I will proclaim your righteousness to others.

Your work is honorable and glorious, and your righteousness endures forever. Thank you, Father. Open to me the gates of righteousness, and I will go through them, and I will praise you. Quicken me in your righteousness.

I thank you, Father, that your righteousness is an

everlasting righteousness, and your law is the truth. The righteousness of your testimonies is everlasting. Give me understanding, and I shall live. My tongue shall speak of your Word, for I know that all your commandments consist of righteousness.

Hear my prayer, O Lord. Give ear to my supplications. Answer me in your faithfulness and righteousness. Help me to ever declare your greatness, your goodness, and your righteousness. Thank you for always being gracious and full of compassion, my Lord. You are slow to anger and of great mercy. Thank you for your goodness and your tender mercies.

In the name of the Righteous One I pray, Amen.

Scriptures: Psalm 4; Psalm 7; Psalm 11; Psalm 15; Psalm 17; Psalm 23; Psalm 35; Psalm 37; Psalm 71; Psalm 111; Psalm 118; Psalm 119; Psalm 143; Psalm 145.

Personal Affirmation: I will walk in God's righteousness from this time forward. His righteousness shall be a shield for me.

New Testament Scripture: "If ye know that he is righteous, ye know that every one that doeth righteousness is born of him" (1 John 2:29).

Reflection: *"The Son of God became a man to enable men to become sons of God"* (C.S. Lewis).

37

SALVATION—
OUR COMPLETION IN CHRIST

Salvation belongeth unto the Lord:
thy blessing is upon thy people.
(Psalm 3:8)

Central Truth: Salvation can only be found through Jesus Christ. He is the King of kings, the Lord of lords, and our Savior.

Central Focus: The salvation that God gives to us through His grace sets us free from Satan, sin, and darkness. Praise God for the redemption and salvation we have through Jesus Christ, our Lord.

Prayer: Heavenly Father, thank you for saving me through your Son. I rejoice in your salvation. I will ever love you, O Lord my strength. You are my rock, my fortress, and my deliverer. You are my God and my strength, and I will ever trust in you. Thank you for being my buckler and the horn of my salvation. You are my high tower, dear Lord.

Thank you for girding me with strength and making my way perfect. You have made my feet like hinds' feet, and you have set me upon high places. Thank you, Father. I praise you that you have taught my hands to war, so that a bow of steel is broken by my arms. Hallelujah! I will ever call upon you, O Lord, for you are worthy to be praised, and so shall I be saved from all my enemies.

You have given me the shield of your salvation, and your right hand holds me up. Your gentleness has made me great. Thank you, Father. Show me your ways, O Lord, and teach me your paths. Lead me in your truth and teach me, for you are the God of my salvation, and I wait on you throughout the day.

You, O Lord, are my light and my salvation. Whom shall I fear? You are the strength of my life. Of whom should I be afraid? I will fear no one, Lord, because you are my salvation, and I shall ever thank you. Create in me a clean heart, O God, and renew a right spirit within me. Do not cast me away from your presence. Do not take your Holy Spirit from me. Restore unto me the joy of your salvation, and uphold me with your free spirit.

Truly, my soul waits for you, Lord God. My salvation comes from you. You only are my rock and my salvation. You are also my defense. As a result, I know I shall not be moved. Blessed are you, O God. Daily you load me with benefits, and you are the God of my salvation. Thank you so much for all you have done, are doing, and will do for me.

Father, I will hope continually in you, and I will praise you more and more. My mouth will show forth your righteousness and your salvation all the day long. I love you, Father.

In the Savior's name I pray, Amen.

Scriptures: Psalm 9; Psalm 18; Psalm 25; Psalm 27; Psalm 51; Psalm 62; Psalm 68.

Personal Affirmation: I will proclaim the salvation of the Lord to others, and I will thank God for the wonder of eternal life through Jesus Christ, my Lord.

New Testament Scripture: "Who are kept by the power of God through faith unto salvation ready to be revealed in the last time" (1 Peter 1:5).

Reflection: *"All our salvation consists in the manifestation of the nature, life, and spirit of Jesus Christ in our inward new man. This alone is Christian redemption, this alone delivers from the guilt and power of sin, this alone redeems and renews"* (William Law).

38

SEEKING THE LORD— A HIGH PRIORITY FOR EACH BELIEVER

The Lord looked down from heaven upon the children of men, to see if there were any that did understand, and seek God.

(Psalm 14:2)

Central Truth: If we seek God, we will find Him.

Central Focus: Seeking the Lord results in great blessing and favor in our lives. As we seek Him, we will be found by Him and we will learn His ways and experience all He has for us.

Prayer: Father, I seek you with all my heart. My praise shall be of you in the great congregation. Help me to be meek, for I know the meek shall eat and be satisfied. I will praise you as I seek you, Lord, and I know my heart will live on.

One thing have I desired of you, Lord, and that I will continue to seek after: that I may dwell in your house all the days of my life and behold your beauty forever and to inquire in your temple. Thank you, Father, for your promise to me that assures me that you will hide me in your pavilion in times of trouble. I know you will set me upon a rock.

When your voice tells me to seek your face, my heart

declares, "Your face will is seek, O Lord." Do not hide your face from me, for you are my help. Teach me your way, O Lord, and lead me in a plain path. As I wait on you, good courage builds within me and you are strengthening my heart. Thank you, Lord.

It thrills me to know that when I seek you, Lord, I will not want any good thing, for you supply all my needs. Hallelujah! Seeking you causes me to rejoice, Father, and I will ever be glad in you. I love your salvation, and I shall say continually, "The Lord be magnified."

O God, you are my God, and I will seek you early each morning. My soul thirsts for you and my flesh longs for you in a dry and thirsty land where there is no water. Your loving-kindness is greater than life to me. My lips shall praise you, and I will bless you while I live, and I will lift up my hands in your name.

Lord God, I seek you and your strength. I will seek your face forevermore and remember your marvelous works, your wonders, and the judgments of your mouth. It brings great blessing into my life when I keep your testimonies and seek you with all my heart.

Father, I walk in liberty as I seek your precepts. I will speak of your testimonies, and I shall not be ashamed. I will delight myself in your commandments, which I greatly love. I was glad when they said unto me, "Let us go into the house of the Lord." I will seek your good, Lord.

Unto you, O God, do I lift up my eyes, for you dwell in the heavens. Have mercy upon me, O Lord, have mercy upon me. My help is in your name, O Lord, for I know you have made both Heaven and Earth. I am very blessed as I fear you and walk in your ways. Help me to do so at all times.

I will praise you with my whole heart, O God. I will sing and give praise to you all the time. I will worship toward your holy temple and praise your name forever. I thank you for your loving-kindness and your truth, for you have magnified your Word above your name. I love your Word, Father, for it is a lamp unto my feet and a light unto my path.

I will seek to follow your Word each step of my way.

In Jesus' name I pray, Amen.

Scriptures: Psalm 22; Psalm 27; Psalm 34; Psalm 40; Psalm 63; Psalm 105; Psalm 119; Psalm 122; Psalm 123; Psalm 124; Psalm 128; Psalm 138.

Personal Affirmation: Seeking the Lord and His truth will become one of my highest priorities throughout my life.

New Testament Scripture: "But seek ye first the kingdom of God, and his righteousness; and all these things shall be added unto you" (Matthew 6:33).

Reflection: *"Let God's promises shine on your problems"* (Corrie ten Boom).

39

STRENGTH—
A GOD-GIVEN QUALITY

*I will love thee, O Lord, my strength. The Lord is my
rock, and my fortress, And my deliverer; my God,
my strength, in whom I will trust; my buckler, and
the horn of my salvation, and my high tower.*

(Psalm 18:1-2)

Central Truth: My strength comes from God. Indeed,
He is my strength.

Central Focus: I am strong in the Lord and in the power
of His might.

Prayer: O Lord, my strength, I give my life afresh to
you. Dear God, I thank you that you always gird me
with strength and make my way perfect. Thank you
for making my feet like hinds' feet and for setting me
on high places.

Let the words of my mouth and the meditation of my
heart be acceptable in your sight, O Lord, my strength
and my Redeemer. I joy in your strength, O Lord. You
have given me my heart's desire and you have not
withheld the requests of my lips. I praise you, Father.

Lord God, you are my light and my salvation. Whom
shall I fear? You are the strength of my life. Of whom
shall I be afraid? Lord, you are my strength and my
shield. My heart totally trusts in you. You have greatly

helped me. Therefore, my heart greatly rejoices. With my song I will praise you.

You are the God of my strength, O Lord. O send out your light and your truth, and let them lead me. Let them bring me unto your holy hill and to your tabernacles. You are my refuge and my strength, dear Father, and you are a very present help in trouble. Therefore, I will not fear, though the Earth be removed and the mountains be cast into the sea. You are always with me. Praise your matchless name!

I will ever sing of your power, O God, and I will sing aloud of your mercy in the morning, for you have been my defense and refuge in the day of trouble. Unto you, O my strength, will I sing, for you are my defense and the God of my mercy.

I will seek you, O God, and your strength. I will seek your face forevermore, as I remember your marvelous works and your wonders. You are the Lord, my God, and I love you so much. You have always helped me, Father, and I praise your holy name. You will always be my strength and song, and I thank your for your great salvation.

Father, I will praise you with my whole heart. I will worship you and praise your name. Thank you for your loving-kindness, your truth, and your strength. Thank you for strengthening me with strength in my soul. Blessed are you, my strength. Thank you for teaching my hands to war and my fingers to fight. You are my goodness, my fortress, my high tower, my deliverer, and my shield. I trust in you, O Lord.

I will wait on you, O Lord, and I will be of good courage, for you are strengthening my heart. Thank you for giving your great strength to me.

In the strong name of Jesus I pray, Amen.

Scriptures: Psalm 18; Psalm 19; Psalm 21; Psalm 27; Psalm 28; Psalm 43; Psalm 46; Psalm 59; Psalm 105; Psalm 118; Psalm 138; Psalm 144.

Personal Affirmation: Through God I will go from strength to strength. It is strength that enables me to accomplish great things through Him.

New Testament Scripture: "I can do all things through Christ which strengtheneth me" (Philippians 4:13).

Reflection: *"If God brings you to it, He will bring you through it"* (Anonymous).

40
TEACHING—
LEARNING GOD'S WAYS

Shew me thy ways, O Lord; teach me thy paths.
Lead me in thy truth, and teach me:
for thou are the God of my salvation;
on thee do I wait all the day.
(Psalm 25:4-5)

Central Truth: God's ways are perfect, and He teaches me His ways through His Word.

Central Focus: God is teaching me every day, and He is showing me how to live my life. I wait upon Him, and I know He will reveal His truth to me. He is the God of my salvation, my teacher, and my Lord.

Prayer: O God, my Father, lead me in your truth and teach me. Remember, O Lord, your tender mercies and loving-kindnesses, for they have been ever of old. Praise you, Lord.

Guide me in judgment and teach me your ways in everything. I thank you for the truth that your secret is with those who fear you. Thank you for your promise that you will reveal your covenant to me. I love you, O Lord, my God.

Teach me your way, O Lord, and lead me in a plain path because of my enemies. As I wait on you, I am greatly encouraged, for I know you are strengthening my heart. Hallelujah!

Thank you, Lord, for instructing me and teaching me in the way wherein I should go. Thank you for guiding me with your eye. I will be glad in you and rejoice for all your goodness to me.

Thank you for your promise which tells me that you will teach me how to fear you. I want always to respect and honor you, Father. Teach me your way, and I will walk in your truth. Unite my heart to fear your name.

Teach me to number my days, O Lord, so that I will be able to apply my heart to wisdom. Teach me your statutes, Father. Teach me the way of your statutes, and I will keep them until the end. Give me understanding, and I shall keep your law. Father, it is my desire to observe it with my whole heart.

Make me to go in the path of your commandments, for I find my delight in them. Incline my heart to your testimonies, and turn my eyes away from vanities. Quicken me in your way, and establish your Word in my life.

Father, I ask that you would teach me good judgment and knowledge, for I believe in your commandments. Cause me to hear your loving-kindness in the mornings, for I put my complete trust in you, O Lord. Cause me to know the way wherein I should walk, for I lift up my soul to you.

Teach me to do your will, O Lord, for your name's sake. Blessed are you, O Lord, my strength. Thank you for teaching my hands to war and my fingers to fight. You are my goodness, my fortress, my high tower, my deliverer, and my shield, and I will ever trust in you.

Thank you for teaching me, O Lord.

Scriptures: Psalm 25; Psalm 27; Psalm 32; Psalm 34; Psalm 86; Psalm 90; Psalm 119; Psalm 143; Psalm 143; Psalm 144.

Personal Affirmation: Where He leads me I will follow. What He teaches to me I will obey. What He shows to me, I will do, and what He tells me, I will heed. He is my Master, and I am His follower.

New Testament Scripture: "Study to shew thyself approved unto God, a workman that needeth not to be ashamed, rightly dividing the word of truth" (2 Timothy 2:15).

Reflection: *"We have one function in life: to be the manifestors of His life to the world. Only when we are living His life are we truly living our own"* (Malcolm Smith).

41

THANKSGIVING— THE RESPONSE OF A HEART TOUCHED BY GOD

Sing unto the Lord with thanksgiving. Sing praise upon the harp unto our God.
(Psalm 147:7)

Central Truth: Thanksgiving is a way of life for the believer. We are so blessed to know the Lord, and it is thrilling to know how much He has done for us. Thanking Him is one of the best ways we have of showing our love for Him.

Central Focus: Counting my blessings is so important. It keeps me focused on the things that are positive and it draws me closer to God—the Giver of every good and perfect gift.

Prayer: Lord God, I offer unto you thanksgiving, as I pay my vows unto you, the Most High God of the universe. As I call upon you, I know you will deliver me. I want to glorify you with my life. I will praise you with my song, Father, and I will magnify you with thanksgiving.

My heart sings unto you, O Lord, as I make a joyful noise unto you, the God of my salvation. I come before your presence with thanksgiving, and I make a joyful noise unto you with Psalms, for you are a great God and a great King above all gods. In your hand are the deep places of the Earth. The strength of the hills is yours also. The sea is yours, and your hands formed the dry land. I worship and bow down before you; I kneel before you, Lord, for you are my Maker and my God. I am but a sheep in your pasture.

It is my pleasure to serve you with gladness and to come before your presence with singing. I know that you are the Lord, my God. I enter your gates with thanksgiving and I go into your courts with praise. I am very thankful to you, Father, and I bless your holy name, for you are good and your mercy is everlasting. Your truth endures to all generations.

I praise you for your goodness and for your wonderful works. I offer unto you the sacrifice of thanksgiving, and I declare your works with rejoicing. I love you, Lord, because you have heard my voice and my supplications. Thank you for inclining your ear toward me. I will call upon you for as long as I live.

Thank you for delivering my soul from death, my eyes from tears, and my feet from falling. I will walk before you in the land of the living. It is good to sing praises to you, O Lord. It is very pleasant indeed. Thank you for healing my broken heart and for binding up my wounds.

I sing unto you with thanksgiving, and I praise your holy name. Thank you for strengthening the bars of my gates and giving me your peace.

Thank you for everything, my God. Thank you for

what you have done, are doing, and will do in my life. Hallelujah!

Scriptures: Psalm 50; Psalm 69; Psalm 95; Psalm 100; Psalm 116; Psalm 147.

Personal Affirmation: I will thank the Lord at all times and bless His holy name.

New Testament Scripture: "In every thing give thanks: for this is the will of God in Christ Jesus concerning you" (1 Thessalonians 5:18).

Reflection: *"Weave in faith and God will find the thread"* (Anonymous).

42

TRUST—
CLINGING TO GOD

Blessed are all they that put their trust in him.
(Psalm 2:12)

Central Truth: Trusting the Lord is so important. Our attitude needs to be like that of Job: "Though he slay me, yet will I trust in him" (Job 13:15).

Central Focus: I want to learn how to truly trust the Lord with everything in my life, to cling to Him in total dependency, for I need Him at all times. Therefore, I will trust Him fully, without leaning upon my own understanding. In doing so, I know He will direct my steps. (See Proverbs 3:5–6.)

Prayer: I trust you, O Lord, my God. I offer unto you the sacrifice of righteousness, as I put all my trust in you. I rejoice as I put my trust in you, Father, and I will ever shout for joy, because I know you are defending me. I love you and I love your name. Thank you for blessing me with your favor as with a shield.

O Lord my God, in you do I put my trust. Save me from all who would persecute me and deliver me. Thank you for being my refuge in times of trouble. I know your name, and I put my trust in you. Preserve me, O God, for in you do I put my trust. Thank you for showing me the path of life. In your presence there is fullness of joy, and at your right hand there are pleasures forevermore. Thank you so much, Father.

Continue to show me your marvelous loving-kindness, Lord, for you have saved me by your right hand. I put my complete trust in you. Keep me as the apple of your eye, and hide me under the shadow of your wings. I will love you, O Lord, my strength. You are my rock and my fortress. You are my Deliverer and my God. You are my strength in whom I trust. You are my buckler and the horn of my salvation. I praise you, mighty God.

Some trust in chariots and some in horses, but I will remember your name, O Lord. Unto you, O Lord, do I lift up my soul. O my God, I trust in you. Do not let me be ashamed, and do not let my enemies triumph over me. Show me your ways, O Lord, and teach me your paths. Lead me in your truth and teach me, for you are the God of my salvation, and I wait upon you all day long.

In you I put my trust, O Lord. Be my strong rock and a house of defense to save me. You are my rock and my fortress. Therefore, for your name's sake lead me and guide me. I will trust in you and do good, Father, and I will delight in you. Thank you for your promise to give me the desires of my heart. I commit my way to you, and I trust in you. Therefore, I know you will bring it to pass in my life.

I am like a green olive tree in your house, O God, and I will trust in your mercy forever and ever. Whenever I am tempted to be afraid, I will trust in you. I will praise your Word, and I will trust in you. In doing so, I will not fear anyone or anything.

In you, O Lord, I put my trust. Let me never be put to confusion. Deliver me in your righteousness and cause me to escape. Incline your ear to me, and save me. Be my strong habitation, Father, whereunto I will continually resort. You are my hope, O Lord God, and you have been my trust since my youth.

I know it is better to trust in you, Lord, than to place my confidence in human beings. You are my God, and I will praise you and exalt you forever.

Thank you for giving me the grace to trust you, Father.

Scriptures: Psalm 4; Psalm 5; Psalm 7; Psalm 9; Psalm 11; Psalm 16; Psalm 17; Psalm 18; Psalm 20; Psalm 25; Psalm 31; Psalm 37; Psalm 52; Psalm 56; Psalm 71; Psalm 118.

Personal Affirmation: I will trust the Lord at all times. I will cling to Him every minute. I will believe His Word and live by its precepts.

New Testament Scripture: "That we should be to the praise of his glory, who first trusted in Christ, in whom ye also trusted, after that ye heard the word of truth, the gospel of your salvation" (Ephesians 1:12, 13).

Reflection: *"Learn to know Christ and Him crucified. Learn to sing to Him and say, 'Lord Jesus, you are my righteousness; I am your sin. You have taken upon yourself what is mine and given me what is yours. You have become what you were not so that I might become what I was not"* (Martin Luther).

43
WISDOM—
A GIFT OF GOD

*The law of the Lord is perfect, converting the soul:
the testimony of the Lord is sure, Making wise the
simple. The statutes of the Lord are right, rejoicing
the heart: the Commandment of the Lord is pure,
enlightening the eyes.*

(Psalm 19:7-8)

Central Truth: God's wisdom is to be greatly desired, because it is the source of so many good things. To be wise we must fear the Lord and follow His ways.

Central Focus: The Lord Jesus Christ who lives within us is our wisdom. It is He who makes us wise, and His grace enables us to walk in wisdom each step of the way.

Prayer: God, you are so wise and so wonderful. I come to you now, seeking your wisdom for my life. May your righteousness in my life enable me to speak wisdom at all times, and may my tongue speak your judgments.

My mouth shall speak of wisdom and the meditations of my heart shall be of understanding. Father, I know you desire truth in my inner parts, and so I ask you to help me know wisdom deep within. Purge me with hyssop and I shall be clean. Wash me, and I shall be whiter than snow.

Make me to hear joy and gladness. Create in me a clean heart, O God, and renew a right spirit within me. Cast me not away from your presence, and do not take your Holy Spirit from me. Restore unto me the joy of your salvation and uphold me with your free spirit.

Teach me to number my days, that I would apply my heart to wisdom. O Lord, how manifold are your works. You have made them all in wisdom, and the earth is full of your riches. Thank you, Father. I realize, dear Father, that wisdom stems from fearing and respecting you. Thank you for the good understanding you have given to me through your commandments. Your praise shall endure forever.

Your law, O Lord, is perfect and it converts the soul. Your testimony is sure, and it makes the simple wise. Your statutes are right, and they rejoice my heart. Your commandments are pure, and they enlighten my eyes. The fear of you is clean, and it endures forever. Your judgments are true and righteous altogether.

I realize, dear Lord, that they are more to be desired than gold, and they are sweeter than the honeycomb. Thank you, Father. Keeping your commandments brings great reward to me, Lord. Cleanse me from secret faults and keep me from presumptuous sins. Let them not have dominion over me. Let the words of my mouth and the meditation of my heart be acceptable in your sight, O Lord, my strength and my Redeemer.

Thank you for the wisdom you've imparted to me, Father. I will walk in wisdom by observing your Word and its precepts. As a result, I know I will understand your loving-kindness more fully.

Praise you, Father.

In Jesus' name I pray, Amen.

Scriptures: Psalm 37; Psalm 49; Psalm 51; Psalm 90; Psalm 104; Psalm 111; Psalm 19; Psalm 107.

Personal Affirmation: I will walk in wisdom from this day forth.

New Testament Scripture: "In whom we have redemption through his blood, the forgiveness of sins, according to the riches of his grace; Wherein he hath abounded toward us in all wisdom and prudence" (Ephesians 1:7-8).

Reflection: *"I, as a human, do not become the power or love or wisdom of God; I merely contain Him who is all these, and everything"* (Norman Grubb).

44

WORSHIP— ENTERING GOD'S PRESENCE

Give unto the Lord the glory due unto his name;
worship the Lord in the beauty of holiness.
(Psalm 29:2)

Central Truth: God is worthy of all our worship.

Central Focus: I will learn how to worship God in the beauty of holiness, to worship Him in spirit and truth, and to worship Him for who He is.

Prayer: O God, my heavenly Father, I draw near to you, and, as I do so, I know you are drawing near to me. I come into your presence in the multitude of your mercies, and I will honor you and worship you. Lead me, O Lord, in your righteousness and make your way straight before my face. Thank you, Lord.

All the Earth shall worship you and sing unto you. They will sing in your name. You are so great, and you do wonders. You alone are God. Teach me your way, O Lord. I will walk in your truth. Unite my heart to fear your name. I will praise you, O Lord my God, with my whole heart. I will glorify your name forevermore.

Thank you for your great mercy to me. You are a God who is full of compassion. You are gracious, patient, and plenteous in mercy and truth. Thank you, Father. Turn unto me, and have mercy upon me.

Give your strength to me. Thank you for helping and comforting me.

I come unto you with singing, Father, and I will ever make a joyful noise unto you, for you are the rock of my salvation. I come before your presence with thanksgiving, and I make a joyful noise unto you with Psalms. You, O Lord, are a great God, and you are a great King above all gods. Hallelujah!

I worship and bow down before you. I kneel before you, O Lord, my Maker. You are my God. I am but a sheep in your pasture. I wait before you, and I listen for your voice. I sing a new song unto you. I bless your holy name. You are so great and you are greatly to be praised.

Honor and majesty go before you, and strength and beauty are in your tabernacle. I worship you, Abba-Father. You reign above us, O Lord. I praise your great and terrible name, for it is holy. I exalt you, Lord God, and I worship at your footstool, for you are holy.

I exalt you and I worship at your holy hill, for you are holy, O God, my Lord. I will praise you with my whole heart, O God, and I will worship toward your holy temple. I will praise your name for your loving-kindness and your truth. Thank you for magnifying your Word above your name.

In the day when I cried you answered me and you strengthened me with strength in my soul. Great is your glory, O Lord. When I walk in the midst of trouble, I know you will revive me. You will stretch forth your hand against the wrath of my enemies, and your right hand will save me.

Thank you for your wonderful promise that you will perfect that which concerns me. Your mercy endures forever, O Lord.

I will worship you every day of my life.

In Jesus' name, Amen.

Scriptures: Psalm 5; Psalm 66; Psalm 86; Psalm 95; Psalm 96; Psalm 98; Psalm 99.

Personal Affirmation: I love to worship the Lord, and I will do so at all times. I will practice His presence through worship and praise.

New Testament Scripture: "God is a Spirit: and they that worship him must worship him in spirit and in truth" (John 4:24).

Reflection: *"Here lies the tremendous mystery—that God should be all-powerful, yet refuse to coerce. He summons us to cooperation. We are honored in being given the opportunity to participate in His good deeds. Remember how he asked for help in performing His miracles? Fill the waterpots, stretch out your hand, distribute the loaves"* (Elisabeth Elliot).

PART VIII

GOD WILL TAKE CARE OF YOU

(PRAYER BASED ON PSALM 91)

I will say of the Lord, He is my refuge and my
fortress: my God; in him will I trust.
(Psalm 91:2)

Because we have set our love upon the Lord, we know He will deliver us. Many use Psalm 91, sometimes called "the Psalm of Protection," to call out to God in times of hardship. It is a marvelous and precious promise from God that He will take care of you—no matter what.

Prayer: Dear Lord, thank you for being my refuge and my fortress. Thank you for taking me under your wing and covering me with your feathers. Thank you for shielding me with your truth.

I am not afraid. Terror that comes by night, arrows or weapons that fly through the air in the daytime, disease or pestilence that come with darkness, or destruction that lays waste even at noontime—none of these make me afraid, for I abide under your shadow.

Though a thousand fall at my side and ten thousand at my right hand, I fear not. You are my protection.

I do not fear evil, or plague, or death itself, for I know you have given your angels charge over me, to keep me in all your ways. You have shown me your salvation.

I love you so much, Father, and I set my love upon you. Thank you for your promise of deliverance. Thank you, also, for your promise to set me on high, because I know your name. I treasure your name, Lord. When I call upon you, I know you will answer me, and I know you will always be with me, even in times of trouble. Praise your holy name!

Thank you, Father, for delivering me, honoring me, and satisfying me with long life. Thank you for showing me your salvation. I claim your promises now in Jesus' name. I know you will always take care of me.

GOD WILL TAKE CARE OF YOU

*(Words by Civilla D. Martin;
music by Walter S. Martin, 1904)*

Be not dismayed whate'er betide,
God will take care of you;
Beneath His wings of love abide,
God will take care of you.

No matter what may be the test,
God will take care of you;
Lean, weary one, upon His breast,
God will take care of you.

Through every day, o'er all the way;
God will take care of you.